GHOST TOWNS OF THE
AMERICAN WEST

GHOST TOWNS

OF THE

AMERICAN WEST

BY

Robert Silverberg

ILLUSTRATED BY

Lorence Bjorklund

OHIO UNIVERSITY PRESS   ATHENS

Library of Congress Cataloging-in-Publication Data

Silverberg, Robert.
Ghost towns of the American West/ by Robert Silverberg;
illustrated by Lorence Bjorklund.
p. cm.
Originally published: New York: Crowell, [1968].
Includes bibliographical references (p.) and index.
ISBN 0-8214-1082-2 (paperback)
1. Ghost towns – West (U.S.)
2. Mines and mineral resources – West (U.S.) – History.
3. West (U.S.) – History, Local.   I. Title.
F591.S55   1994

978--dc20   93-47111
                                                         CIP

Text designed by Joan Maestro
Cover designed by Chiquita Babb
Printed in the United States of America

Ohio University Press books are printed on acid-free paper ∞
First Ohio University Press paperback edition printed 1994

99 98 97 96 95 94   5 4 3 2 1

Ohio University Press, Athens, Ohio 45701

Contents

GHOST TOWNS OF THE AMERICAN WEST

ONE

Golden Ghosts

A FEW CRUMBLING BUILDINGS stand beside an unpaved road overgrown with sagebrush. Paint and plaster
long since have vanished; bare timbers are exposed to
the harshness of the western sun and the fierceness of
the winter gales. This shattered ruin was once a bank
where weary miners stood in line to deposit their new
wealth. This gaunt hovel beside it used to be a wild
saloon, alive with the sounds of singing and carousing,
the jangling chords of a honkytonk piano, the grunts
of poker players, the occasional blasts of gunfire. Over
here was a grand hotel, but the red carpets and glittering chandeliers disappeared long ago, and the last champagne cork was popped here when Teddy Roosevelt
was in the White House. These dimly seen lines in the
ground mark the foundations of houses, for there was
a time when five thousand people lived in this town.

That narrow path winding into the mountains leads to the mines . . . the mines whose gold made this town sprout overnight.

When the gold gave out, the town died. The yellow metal no longer came forth, and the miners drifted away, off to seek treasure in more likely quarters. The population dropped slowly but steadily, until only the diehards remained, those who still felt there was life in the mines. A hundred and· fifty people hung on in what had been a town of thousands. Windows broke and never were repaired. Wild creatures moved into the abandoned cabins. The gravestones of heroes toppled in the town cemetery, and the names of the heroes were forgotten. In time the hard core of settlers also moved away, leaving just the dead husk of the town.

No one has ever counted the ghost towns of the American West. A true census is impossible, for hundreds of them have gone without a trace, completely obliterated by time and the elements. No western state is without its ghost towns, those poignant reminders of an America never to return. They were cities of dreams—mining camps that sprang up during the great gold rushes of the nineteenth century, grew with sudden furious energy, enjoyed a decade or two of gaudy life, and then faded and perished. From the parched deserts of Arizona and New Mexico to the high plateau of Oregon, from the Sierra Nevada country of Cali-

fornia to the Dakota Badlands, these relics of the pio-
neering days mark the excitement and gaiety of the
boom-time era of the old West.

There are degrees of ghostliness among the ghost
towns. Not every mining camp met the same sort of
death, and some did not die at all. The mines are still
going strong in places like Butte, Montana, and Globe,
Arizona; a few traces of the old days are visible, but
these have become modern cities, very much alive. In
some of the other early mining towns, the mines have
played out, but other industries have developed: farming, cattle raising, lumbering, or, as in the cases of Virginia City, Nevada, and Tombstone, Arizona, tourism.
In these places many of the original buildings of the
gold-rush days are carefully preserved to attract visitors.

Then there are the partial ghost towns, such as Goldfield, Nevada, and Deadwood, South Dakota, where
sections of the town are still inhabited and some mining
still is done, but where the early buildings survive like
windows into yesterday. And there are the true ghost
towns, wholly deserted or perhaps inhabited by one or
two families—stark, somber collections of tumbledown
shacks, withering into nothingness, sleeping their final
sleep. Bodie, California, and Bullfrog, Nevada, belong
in this class. Lastly, there are the mining camps that the
scythe of time has completely cut away. Nothing at
all remains, except perhaps the stump of a building

jutting above the barren soil or the shadowy outlines of vanished streets. Typical ghosts of this sort are Silver Reef, Utah, and Charleston, Arizona.

All these ghost towns are the heritage of the mining booms that began in 1849 in California, when men from all over the world stampeded toward the Sierra Nevada Mountains in search of quick wealth. Some of those who went West in '49 achieved great fortunes; most did not, and turned away, disappointed but always optimistic, ready to follow any rumor of a gold discovery. Fickle and easily tempted, these prospectors rarely stayed in one place long. Towns sprang up and grew like mushrooms while the mining was good, but they could perish as easily as they had been founded. The pattern was repeated again and again: a strike of gold, an influx of miners, the birth of a bustling camp. Then came those who hoped to get rich serving the miners: the saloonkeepers, the bankers, the laundrymen, the grocery-store operators, the surveyors and engineers, the gamblers. Presto, a mining camp became a town! A town became a city! Within three or four years, a collection of tents might turn into a metropolis with an opera house, a sumptuous hotel, a row of thriving shops. And then the flow of treasure from the earth slackened, or someone came into town with tales of even easier wealth somewhere else. Off the miners went, laughing, quarreling, predicting bonanzas in the next range of mountains, leaving behind a dying town. Perhaps later on, other prospectors would come and find new treasure there—silver or copper instead of gold, maybe—and a second cycle of feverish growth would begin. Some of the mining camps went through three or four lifetimes this way before sinking into their last slumber.

It did not take long for these ghost towns to begin appearing. By the end of 1850 California was dotted with mining camps that had played out fast. The village of Washington, California, on the Yuba River, had a lifetime of little more than a year; what had seemed to be a rich strike of gold turned out otherwise, and the miners departed, leaving behind their cabins and stores and a large hotel. The story was a common one. Mark Twain, who lived in California and Nevada during some of the liveliest years of the mining boom, described the abandoned mines of California's Sacramento Valley in his book *Roughing It*, published in 1871:

> It was in this Sacramento Valley . . . that a deal of the most lucrative of the early gold-mining was done, and you may still see, in places, its grassy slopes and levels torn and guttered and disfigured by the avaricious spoilers of fifteen and twenty years ago. You may see such disfigurements far and wide over California—and in some such places, where only meadows and forests are visible—not a living creature, not a house, no stick or stone or remnant of a ruin, and not a sound, not even a whisper to disturb the Sabbath stillness—you will find it hard to believe that there stood at one time a fiercely flourishing little city, of two thousand or three thousand

souls, with its newspaper, fire company, brass band, volunteer militia, bank, hotels, noisy Fourth-of-July processions and speeches, gambling-hells crammed with tobacco-smoke, profanity, and rough-bearded men of all nations and colors, with tables heaped with gold-dust sufficient for the revenues of a German principality— streets crowded and rife with business—town lots worth four hundred dollars a front foot—labor, laughter, music, dancing, swearing, fighting, shooting, stabbing—a bloody inquest and a man for breakfast every morning— *everything* that delights and adorns existence—all the appointments and appurtenances of a thriving and prosperous and promising young city—and *now* nothing is left of it but a lifeless, homeless solitude. The men are gone, the houses have vanished, even the *name* of the place is forgotten. In no other land, in modern times, have towns so absolutely died and disappeared, as in the old mining regions of California.

Those who came looking for gold drew this ringing epitaph from Mark Twain:

It was a driving, vigorous, restless population in those days. It was a *curious* population. It was the *only* population of the kind that the world has ever seen gathered together, and it is not likely that the world will ever see its like again. For, observe, it was an assemblage of two hundred thousand *young* men—not simpering, dainty, kid-gloved weaklings, but stalwart, muscular, dauntless young braves, brimful of push and energy, and royally endowed with every attribute that goes to make up a peerless and magnificent manhood—the very pick and choice of the world's glorious ones. No women, no children, no gray and stooping veterans—none but erect, bright-eyed, quick moving, strong-handed young giants —the strangest population, the finest population, the most gallant host that ever trooped down the startled solitudes of an unpeopled land. And where are they now? Scattered to the ends of the earth—or prematurely aged and decrepit—or shot and stabbed in street affrays—or dead of disappointed hopes and broken hearts —all gone, or nearly all—victims devoted upon the altar of the golden calf—the noblest holocaust that ever wafted its sacrificial incense heavenward. It is pitiful to think upon.

As Mark Twain once said in another connection, this report is greatly exaggerated. Looking back on his western experiences from a distance of five or six years as he wrote, he saw only the "stalwart, muscular, dauntless young braves," and conveniently forgot about most of the real miners in those early camps, who were ragged, unshaven, unbathed, greedy, uncouth, stained with the juice of chewing tobacco, fond of gambling, drinking, and shedding blood, and all in all something less than "the very pick and choice of the world's glorious ones." Yet there is truth in his romantically exaggerated description. For a short-lived moment, the West was a magnet for restless men of all sorts, whose flamboyant exploits created a new mythology for a new nation. The ghost towns that remain are symbols of a high-spirited, free-wheeling era of gold and glory, and of fearless men who ventured into unknown deserts and mountains to wrest treasure from the earth.

Dreams of gold have obsessed men since early times. Gold is a beautiful metal, heavy and gleaming; it does not rust, it is easily worked into jewelry or coinage, and it is scarce enough to be highly desirable. Three thousand years ago, Phoenician miners quarried gold in Spain. The treasure fleets of King Solomon journeyed down the Red Sea to long lost mines in Tarshish and Ophir. "Men now worship gold to the neglect of the gods," grumbled the Roman poet Propertius. There was never enough gold in circulation to suit man's needs, and so the quest was unending.

In the late fifteenth century, a Genoese navigator named Christopher Columbus heard the tales of the Florentine geographer Toscanelli, who spoke of the fabled cities of the Orient, of the glittering capitals of the Khan of Cathay, of the island of Cipangu, Japan, which was "rich in gold, pearls, and gems: the temples and palaces are roofed with solid gold." Columbus went west looking for Cipangu and Cathay, and unexpectedly stumbled upon two huge continents that blocked the route by sea from Europe to Asia. He found gold, too, but other men reaped the real harvest of the Americas. Cortés conquered the fabulous Aztec kingdom of Mexico and sent cascades of treasure into Spanish coffers. A few years later, Pizarro humbled the proud Incas of

Peru, gaining an even more astonishing bounty of gold. Their successes inspired others, who sought in vain. All during the sixteenth century, deluded men roamed South America in search of El Dorado, a mythical kingdom overflowing with precious metals. Another band of gold-hungry fanatics stumbled into New Mexico, hoping to find the legendary Seven Cities of Cíbola, where the streets were supposedly paved with pure gold. All they found were the mud-walled villages of the Pueblo Indians. Though these early explorers came upon silver mines and occasionally some gold, they never managed to equal the incredible yield of Mexico and Peru. Gradually the gold fever subsided. During the seventeenth, eighteenth, and early nineteenth centuries, much of what is now the western United States was under Spanish rule, and the Spaniards, having given up the quest for treasure, had settled down as ranchers and farmers. Arizona, New Mexico, and California had a few small towns; the rest was untamed wilderness.

In 1821 Mexico gained her independence from Spain, and took control of the American Southwest. The land to the north, sweeping from the Mississippi to the Pacific, belonged to the United States, having come to us in the Louisiana Purchase of 1803, but no one had tried to open mines there; the northern pioneers were trappers and traders dealing in furs. Everyone suspected that the West held great mineral wealth, but in all that vastness there seemed no way to know where to begin looking. There were rumors of gold here, gold there, but only rumors.

The real westward movement began to get under way around 1840. Times were hard east of the Mississippi; the panic of 1837 had paralyzed business throughout the United States, and jobs were difficult to find. An endless frontier beckoned to hungry men. "Oregon fever" and "California fever" became contagious, and trains of covered wagons started to crawl through the immense unknown western lands.

These pioneers were not particularly seeking gold. They wanted a place to settle and raise cattle or crops; they were convinced that beyond the treeless sprawl of the prairies and the bleak dryness of the great deserts there were fertile valleys free for the taking. To Oregon they headed first, since it belonged to the United States; then they started filtering into the Mexican-held lands to the south, which were sparsely populated. The first overland party gathered in Independence, Missouri, in the spring of 1841: 69 men, women, and children, with a total of $100 in cash among them. These people made their way westward for a thousand miles, then split into two groups, one blazing the Oregon Trail northwest and the other finding a route through the deserts of northern Nevada and over the towering Sierra Nevada Mountains into California. By the mid-

1840's, there were about five thousand Americans in Oregon and about one thousand in California. The Oregon settlers were grouped about Lee's Mission in the Willamette Valley. Those in California were concentrated on the lower Sacramento River, where the Swiss adventurer named John Sutter had built a fort.

A mood of expansion swept the United States in those years. Politicians talked of our "manifest destiny" to rule North America from coast to coast. In 1845 the voters sent James Knox Polk to the White House to fulfill this destiny. President Polk moved rapidly and vigorously. In 1845 he brought the independent Republic of Texas into the United States, less than a decade after Texas had broken free from Mexican rule. A year later Polk settled an old boundary dispute with England that put the United States in control of the Oregon Territory, which previously had been claimed in part by Canada. At the same time he engineered a war with Mexico, by which the nation acquired thousands of square miles of land, much of it desert, in the Southwest.

Our manifest destiny had been achieved. What remained now was to get a westward migration of real scope under way. Before long, that migration was triggered by something far more exciting than the hope of finding farming lands in the West. In the spring of 1848, a shopkeeper named Sam Brannan, who kept store on the Sacramento River a few miles below the fort John Sutter had built, appeared in the little port of San Francisco, carrying a bottle of gold dust. Brannan strode down San Francisco's streets, waving the bottle on high and shouting, "Gold! Gold from the American River!"

Gold!

The old dreams of El Dorado were revived. Men looked toward the sunset and saw the glitter of fortune. Seeking pay dirt, the "forty-niners" streamed into California to start the first of the great American gold rushes. The boom was about to begin—the boom that brought incredible wealth to some, hardship and frustration to most, and left behind as its memorials the eerie, romantic ghost towns whose hunted ruins stir our imaginations today.

TWO

The California Gold Rush

THE PLACE WHERE IT STARTED was in California's inland mountain country, on a fork of the American River. Deep in a long valley the river rushes buoyantly out of the mountains, flowing strongly enough to make old John August Sutter think about putting all that rampaging energy to work. Sutter decided to build a sawmill on the American River, and let the swift water supply the power to cut logs into salable timber. He sent his carpenter, James Marshall, out to build the sawmill, and Marshall looked into the river and saw the gleam of gold, and the world went wild. It was that simple. Both Sutter and Marshall had good reason to wish that none of it had ever happened.

Sutter, born in Germany in 1803 of Swiss parents, emigrated to the United States in 1834. He lived in St. Louis for a while, moved on to Oregon, and made a voyage to Hawaii before settling in 1839 in the Sacramento Valley of California. California was then Mexican property, and Sutter took out Mexican citizenship in 1840. A year later he received a grant of seventy-six square miles from California's Mexican authorities, and named his little kingdom New Helvetia, after the ancient Latin name for Switzerland. Near the meeting place of the Sacramento and American rivers, Sutter erected a fort to protect his settlement from the Indians.

Sutter's fort became the nucleus of the small American colony in California. Sutter ran a trading post there, operated farms and ranches, and grew wealthy as a merchant supplying goods to the pioneers who managed to reach California from the East. The five-acre fort, with walls eighteen feet high, was the symbol of Sutter's growing power in the area. Year after year he expanded his influence, hiring Indians to work in his fields and setting up mills to produce flour and lumber. In the fall of 1847 Sutter began construction of a large new flour mill, and to get a dependable supply of lumber with which to build it he decided to put up a new sawmill on the American River. The excess output of the sawmill, Sutter figured, could be sold in the small village of Yerba Buena, on the coast, which was shortly to change its name to San Francisco.

The other ranchers in the area were skeptical of these plans. They called Sutter's mill "Sutter's Folly," just as his original settlement in the Sacramento Valley had been called a folly a few years before. But Sutter was a stubborn man, and he believed in doing things his own way.

To build his sawmill Sutter hired Jim Marshall, a moody, restless wheelwright and carpenter. Marshall had been born in New Jersey in 1812, and at the age of twenty-one had headed west across the mountains to Indiana and Illinois, then to Missouri. There he fell ill, and the doctors thought he had only a year or two to live. A wandering trapper told Marshall of the sunny land of California, where his health would soon be restored, and Marshall moved west again. By the autumn of 1844 he was in Oregon, and the following June he joined a party going south to California. He took a job at Sutter's fort, mending wagons and building spinning wheels and plows, and bought a few acres of his own north of New Helvetia as soon as he had saved a little money. He set up a small ranch, but in 1846 he went off to join the troops that were fighting to drive the Mexicans out of California. When he returned to his ranch in the spring of 1847, he found his cattle gone—lost, stolen, or strayed—and had to go back to work for Sutter. Sutter described him as "one of those visionary men who was always dreaming of something," but respected him for his honesty and his competence as a workman.

With about a dozen men Marshall went about the job of building a dam and sawmill on the American

River. They put together a few log cabins for themselves late in August 1847, and then began constructing a dam to divert water from the river into the millrace, or canal, that led to the wheel of the mill. During the autumn and early winter the dam took shape, the frame of the mill went up, and the men worked with pick, shovel, and powder to build the race. Each night they opened the dam and let water rush into the race to sweep away the debris and soil that the day's blasting and digging had loosened. Gradually the race grew deeper and wider. From time to time Marshall went back to Sutter's fort to report to his employer on the progress of the work.

Toward the end of January 1848, Marshall showed up unexpectedly at the fort. Sutter was surprised to see him, for the carpenter had visited him only the previous week. Sutter wrote:

> It was a rainy afternoon when Mr. Marshall arrived at my office in the Fort, very wet. . . . He told me then that he had some important and interesting news which he wished to communicate secretly to me, and wished me to go with him to a place where we should not be disturbed, and where no listeners could come and hear what we had to say.

Sutter went with him to his private rooms; Marshall asked him to lock the door, but Sutter neglected somehow to do it. Sutter tells how a clerk who had been in another part of the house walked into the room just at the moment when Marshall took a rag from his pocket, showing me the yellow metal: he had about two ounces of it; but how quick Mr. M. put the yellow metal in his pocket again can hardly be described. The clerk came to see me on business, and excused himself for interrupting me, and as soon as he had left I was told, "now lock the doors; didn't I tell you that we might have listeners?". . . . Then Mr. M. began to show me this metal, which consisted of small pieces and specimens, some of them worth a few dollars; he told me that he had expressed his opinion to the laborers at the mill, that this might be gold; but some of them were laughing at him and called him a crazy man, and could not believe such a thing.

Sutter ran some chemical tests on the samples Marshall had brought. Yes: the metal was indeed gold of the finest quality. Greatly excited, Marshall asked Sutter to start out at once with him for the mill site. Sutter replied that it was late in the evening, nearly time for dinner; he invited Marshall to stay for the night, and they would make the journey together in the morning. But Marshall could not wait. Off he went into the heavy rain without eating. Sutter promised to visit the mill in the morning. After breakfast, Sutter departed on the fifty-four-mile trip. It was still raining, and on the way he found Marshall, who had been forced to take shelter for the night anyway, in a pile of brush by the roadside. They rode on to the mill, and soon Sutter was staring into the millrace; the dam was closed and the race was dry, and in the bed of the channel could be seen small pieces of gold.

This is Marshall's own account of his discovery:

> While we were in the habit at night of turning the water through the tail race we had dug for the purpose of widening and deepening the race; I used to go down in the morning to see what had been done by the water through the night; and about half past seven o'clock on or about the 19th of January—I am not quite certain to a day, but it was between the 18th and 20th of that month—1848, I went down as usual, and after shutting off the water from the race I stepped into it, near the lower end, and there, upon the rock, about six inches beneath the surface of the water, I DISCOVERED THE GOLD. I was entirely alone at the time. . . . I then collected four or five pieces and went up to Mr. Scott (who was working at the carpenter's bench making the mill wheel) with the pieces in my hand, and said, "I have found it."
>
> "What is it?" inquired Scott.
>
> "Gold," I answered.
>
> "Oh! no," returned Scott, "that can't be."
>
> I replied positively—"I know it to be nothing else."

The action of the river cutting through the millrace had stripped away the earth to expose the underlying bedrock—and there was gold lying on the rock. Marshall found first some tiny thin flakes, and then substantial nuggets.

Sutter was anything but happy about the discovery. For him, the way to wealth lay in building mills and factories and in developing farms and ranches, not in ripping precious metal from the ground. He knew what would happen to his growing industrial and agricultural empire if a gold craze started. His workmen would desert him and take off for the hills to hunt for fortunes. They would leave his sawmill unfinished; they would abandon his fields and livestock; they would destroy all he had built. Strangers would pour into the region, trampling on his crops and tearing up the soil. "The curse of the thing burst upon my mind," he wrote. "I saw from the beginning how the end would be."

He called his workmen together and asked them to keep the news secret for six more weeks, until his sawmill and flour mill were finished. They agreed to remain silent until then. But it was impossible to suppress such a discovery for long. Sutter himself was the first to spread the word; late in February he wrote a friend to say, "I have made a discovery of a gold mine, which, according to experiments we have made, is extraordinarily rich." About the same time, Sutter sent one of Marshall's workmen, a certain Charles Bennett, to the town of Monterey, where the American military authorities in charge of California had their headquarters. Bennett was entrusted with the vital task of obtaining mining rights in the valley of the American River. Naturally, he was pledged to secrecy; but he was less than halfway to Monterey before the temptation to speak out became irresistible. In the town of Benicia, some sixty miles south of Sutter's fort, Bennett was purchasing supplies at a store when one of the local settlers burst in, shouting that coal had been discovered on the slopes of a mountain nearby. There was an immediate hubbub of excitement. Only Bennett scoffed at the discovery.

"Coal?" he said. "I'll show you some coal—the kind they mine on the American River!" He reached inside his shirt and pulled out a buckskin pouch containing six ounces of gold dust. Unable to stop himself now, he poured forth the whole story.

Sam Brannan, who ran a store near Sutter's fort, learned about the gold strike from a wagon driver who had taken some supplies to the men at the sawmill site. Three men who worked at Sutter's flour mill heard the story from their friend Henry Bigler, who had been helping to build the sawmill. "Keep it to yourselves and do not tell anyone," Bigler wrote, "but gold has been found in the Coloma Valley." They told only a few of their friends, and each of those told only a few others.

By March 7, Sutter was feeling the effects of the spreading rumor. That day he noted in his journal,

The first party of Mormons, employed by me left for washing and digging Gold and very soon all followed, and left me only the sick and the lame behind. And at this time I could say that everybody left me from the Clerk to the Cook. What great Damages I had to suffer in my tannery which was just doing a profitable and extensive business, and the Vats was left filled and a quantity of half finished leather was spoiled, likewise a large quantity of raw hides collected by the farmers and of my own killing. The same thing was in every branch of business which I carried on at the time. I began to harvest my wheat, while others was digging and washing Gold, but even the Indians could not be keeped longer at Work. They was impatient to run to the mines, and other Indians had informed them of the Gold and its Value; and so I had to leave more as ⅔ of my harvest in the fields.

A week later the story was in the newspapers. The March 15, 1848, edition of *The Californian*, San Francisco's first newspaper, ran a small item at the bottom of the third column of the second page:

GOLD MINE FOUND

In the newly made raceway of the Saw Mill recently erected by Captain Sutter on the American Fork, gold has been found in considerable quantities. One person brought thirty dollars worth to New Helvetia, gathered there in a short time. California, no doubt, is rich in mineral wealth; great chances here for scientific capitalists. Gold has been found in every part of the country.

Strangely, this article had almost no impact on the settlers at San Francisco. A few of them drifted eastward into the mountains to take a look, but most chose to ignore the news. The gold rush was still confined almost entirely to the inhabitants of New Helvetia. While John Sutter watched in mounting distress, his men deserted him in troops, leaving his settlement paralyzed. San Francisco did not catch the fever until early May, when Sam Brannan appeared in the little village and let loose the electrifying cry, "Gold! Gold from the American River!"

Now the frenzy took hold. Imagining themselves transformed into millionaires at once, the San Franciscans closed their shops, bought mining equipment, and headed for the hills. San Francisco became a town of women and children. The infection spread to the other settlements on the coast. *The Californian* commented bitterly, "The whole country from San Francisco to Los Angeles and from the seashore to the base of the Sierra Nevada resounds to the sordid cry of gold! Gold!! GOLD!!! while the field is left half-planted, the house half-built, and everything neglected but the manufacture of shovels and pickaxes. . . ." And on June 28, 1848, Thomas Larkin, the American consul at San Francisco, wrote to the Secretary of State in Washington:

Three fourths of the houses in the town on the Bay of San Francisco are deserted . . . every blacksmith, carpenter and lawyer is leaving; brick-yards, saw-mills and ranches are left perfectly alone. A large part of the volunteers at San Francisco and Sonoma have deserted [from the army] . . . vessels are losing their crews . . . both our newspapers are discontinued . . . San Francisco has not a justice of the peace left.

John Sutter was in despair. All of California was descending upon New Helvetia, and the prospectors came like a swarm of locusts, devouring his possessions. The miners, he wrote,

stole the cattle and the horses, they stole the bells from the Fort and the weights from the gates, they stole the hides, and they stole the barrels. . . . I could not shut the gates of my Fort in order to keep them out; they would have broken them down. Talking to them did not do any good. I was alone and there was no law. . . . What a great misfortune was this sudden gold discovery for me! It has just broken up and ruined my hard, restless, and industrious labors. . . .

But the gold rush was merely beginning. News traveled incredibly slowly in those days, and all through 1848 the mining fever was confined almost entirely to California. The rest of the country still knew nothing of what was going on. It took seven months for tales of Sacramento gold to reach New York, and when the news arrived it was not believed, for wild stories of gold strikes in California had been heard before, and nothing had come of them. However, the military administrators of California sent a special courier to Washington by way of the Isthmus of Panama, carrying samples of gold from the diggings amounting to several hundred ounces. This at last was acceptable proof, and on December 5, 1848, President Polk went before Congress to describe the situation. In a message that was speedily reprinted in hundreds of newspapers, the President declared:

> It was known that mines of the precious metals existed to a considerable extent in California at the time of its acquisition. Recent discoveries render it probable that these mines are more extensive and valuable than was anticipated. The accounts of the abundance of gold in that territory are of such an extraordinary character as would scarcely command belief, were they not corroborated by the authentic reports of officers in the public service, who have visited the mineral district, and derived the facts which they detail from personal observation.

There were already more than four thousand prospectors engaged in collecting gold, said the President, and the explorations they had made "warrant the belief that the supply is very large." His speech was an open invitation to seek fortunes in the West. The day after he spoke, a shipload of gold-hunters set sail from Boston, bound for San Francisco via Cape Horn, the southernmost tip of South America. Other ships soon left, some for the voyage round the Horn, others carrying passengers to Panama, where they could make their way by land over the narrow, fever-ridden Isthmus and get a ship to California on the other side. By February of 1849, San Francisco Bay began to fill up with vessels bringing in the would-be miners, who quickly became known as "forty-niners." The crews of these ships generally deserted and headed for the mining district themselves, and so did the soldiers stationed in San Francisco. Some captains had trouble assembling enough sailors to get out of the harbor.

The sea passage to San Francisco was only for the well-to-do. Those who could not afford the fare banded together in groups of twenty or thirty, collected supplies, converted wagons into "prairie schooners," and set out by land. Bayard Taylor, a newspaperman who witnessed the gold rush, wrote:

> The great starting point for this route was Independence, Mo., where thousands were encamped through the month of April, waiting until the grass should be sufficiently high for their cattle, before they ventured on the broad ocean of the Plains. From the first of May to the first of June, company after company took its departure from the frontier of civilization, till the emigrant trail . . . was one long line of mule-trains and wagons.

The wandering Indians of the prairies, frightened and confused by this huge procession, retreated to the back country, so the forty-niners were spared the hardship of Indian raids. But an epidemic of cholera assailed them, and the trail became a highway of graves. Taylor wrote, "It is estimated that about four thousand persons perished from this cause. Men were seized without warning with the most violent symptoms, and instances occurred in which the sufferer was left to die alone by the roadside, while his panic-stricken companions pushed for-

ward, vainly trusting to get beyond the influence of the epidemic."

The survivors who reached the clean air of the Rocky Mountains no longer had to worry about cholera, but other hardships awaited them. They toiled over the steep mountains, occasionally compelled to use their mules and horses for food, and when the pack animals were gone they dined on fried rattlesnakes. Beyond the mountains lay Salt Lake City, where the forty-niners could rest and reprovision, and then came the last and most terrible leg of the journey to California. Some went through the deserts, some went by the mountains; all suffered. Those who stumbled into the mining camps of the Sacramento Valley were hardened by their fearful trials and all the more hungry for instant wealth.

During 1849 about 50,000 prospectors, nearly all men, came to California by various routes. They came not only from the eastern United States, but from Mexico, Chile, Hawaii, and even China. Their numbers mounted steadily; by the middle of 1850 California had a population of 100,000, a fifth of them foreigners, and before the end of 1852 there were 250,000 inhabitants, fifteen times as many as in 1848.

Not all of these were miners. In 1852 there were only about 100,000 men in the mining camps. The rest had come along to do business with the miners. As it happened, those who got richest out of the gold rush were the merchants. Josiah Belden, who opened a store at

San Jose, California, in 1848, was nearly wiped out when everyone in town sped off to the mines. Unable to find customers, Belden went to the mines himself simply as a sightseer. When he returned to San Jose, he learned from the man he had left in charge of his store that "a considerable [part] of the Spanish population, who had been in the mines from San Jose . . . returned to that place, and with their newly acquired wealth had gone into the store to buy goods. . . . They commenced trading at such a rate," Belden wrote, "that I found on my return . . . [that I] had sold out nearly my whole stock of goods." He observed that "money was rather a new thing" for most of the miners, "and having come easy and quickly, they were just as ready to spend it." Within two years he sold his store and retired.

Prices were fantastically high, for California was far from civilization, and most goods had to be shipped from thousands of miles away. The miners, their pockets bulging with gold dust, were willing to pay well for what they craved. Gold was easier to find in California than food, and so the price of flour rose to $800 a barrel, eggs were $3 apiece, vinegar $1 for a 24-ounce bottle. One man wrote home that he had to pay $11 for a jar of pickles and two sweet potatoes, while the cost of a needle and two spools of thread was $7.50.

The only merchant who failed to profit from the situation was John Sutter, who had the misfortune to have settled right in the midst of the mining district.

Thousands of forty-niners swept across his land, ruining him rather than enriching him. "I had not an Idea that people could be so mean, and that they would do a Wholesale business in Stealing," he wrote. Sutter abandoned his fort and withdrew to another ranch. He was forced to sell off most of his land, acre by acre, to pay the lawyers who were trying to save his property from the invaders. Pushed aside by greed, he endured blow upon blow, and when fire destroyed his home in 1865 he gave up California altogether and moved to Washington, D.C., and then to Pennsylvania. He lived on a tiny pension from Congress, and devoted himself to seeking government reimbursement for the property he had lost. His claim, originally for $125,000, was whittled down to $50,000 by Congress, but the final authority to pay him never came through. On June 16, 1880, Congress considered Sutter's claim for the sixteenth time and adjourned without taking action on it. Two days later he died in a Washington hotel room, a bitter, penniless old man, still wearing a ring fashioned from the first gold to be found in the American River.

Jim Marshall's fate was scarcely happier. Just before the gold strike, he had bought some land near the sawmill site. In mid-1849 his ranch was overrun by miners who ignored his "No Trespassing" signs, declared that they had "squatter's rights" to settle there, and proceeded to lay out the streets of the new town of Coloma. Bankrupted, Marshall turned away to wander through the gold country, where he saw men finding more gold in a week than he had earned in a lifetime. He went prospecting himself, but wherever he went he was followed by a horde of hangers-on who believed he had the magic touch; whenever he drove a pick into the ground, these followers suddenly emerged, staked out claims alongside him, and got to work. He wrote, "Before I could prospect the ground, numbers flocked in and commenced seeking all around me, and, as numbers tell, some one would find the lead before me and inform their party, and the ground was claimed. Then I would travel again."

Sutter's memoirs declare that Marshall, "following the guidance of his spirit . . . flitted hither and thither about the foothills. Once he asked me for help, and I gave him one or two horses and a few Indians. But they returned after several weeks very much disgusted and said that they would not go with him any more. . . . The curse of the gold seemed to last on him."

He could find no gold, and he could find no work. He roamed the gold fields like a phantom, tormented by the wild prosperity all about him. For a while he earned a sort of a living by going about the country giving lectures, telling the story of his discovery, but in time people ceased to be interested in that. In 1857 he returned to Coloma, built a little cabin, and supported himself by doing odd jobs as a carpenter. Eventually California granted him a small pension, which he sup-

plemented by selling his autograph to sightseers. He lived on this way until 1885, when he died at the age of seventy-four in complete poverty.

For nearly everyone except Sutter and Marshall, California in the 1850's was a land of gaiety and excitement. San Francisco, which had been reduced almost to a ghost town by the first crazy rush inland to the mines, bounced back and became a mighty city of 100,000 people. Nearly everyone who went prospecting stopped in San Francisco first to buy his equipment, and stopped there afterward to sell his gold. The bankers and merchants of San Francisco thrived on this trade. Richard Henry Dana, who visited San Francisco in 1859, told in wonder of looking from the window of a hotel room

> over the city of San Francisco, with its storehouses, towers, and steeples; its court-houses, theatres, and hospitals; its daily journals; its well-filled professions; its fortresses and lighthouses; its wharves and harbor, with their thousand-ton clipper ships, more in number than London or Liverpool sheltered that day; itself one of the capitals of the American Republic, and the sole emporium of a new world, the awakened Pacific . . . when I saw all these things . . . I could scarcely keep my hold on reality at all, or the genuineness of anything, and seemed to myself like one who had moved in "worlds not realized."

San Francisco was a boom town that outlasted the boom. The gold of the Sacramento Valley gradually played out, but the city on the bay survived temporary economic upheavals, survived fire and even earthquake, and grew more magnificent year by year. Things were more uncertain in the mining camps themselves—places with names like Coffee Gulch, Hog Eye, Hangtown, You Bet, Cut Throat, and Boomo Flat. Their moments of grandeur were brief. Fleatown, Whiskey Gulch, Poison Switch, Shirttail Canyon, and the other little camps could live only as long as the gold lasted. While the going was good, it was fabulously good; once the money stopped flowing, the town died. At the height of the boom, in 1852, California's mines yielded more than $81,000,000 in gold. Within a few years, the annual take was less than a fourth as great. That was still an impressive amount—at no time between 1850 and 1900 was less than $11,000,000 of gold mined—but the sharp drop from the summit meant the death of many towns. The ghosts of those towns still litter the Sacramento Valley and its environs, lingering on as reminders of the frenzied years of the great gold rush.

THREE
California Mining Camps

GOLD USUALLY OCCURS in small traces widely spread over the world, but in some regions geological factors have caused great concentrations of the precious metal to accumulate. California is one of those regions. Eons ago, volcanic action sent hot water swirling along the western slopes of the Sierra Nevada Mountains— water so hot that it carried suspended particles of dissolved gold. The water flushed through the quartz of the mountains, leaving the gold behind and creating a giant lode, or deposit, of gold nearly two hundred miles long.

The gold was intricately entangled with the quartz in which it lay. Narrow veins were woven through the quartz in threads and bands, creating a glittering lace of metal. Wind and rain and frost went to work on the rock, splitting it, wearing it down, cutting away the upper layers. It took millions of years, but eventually the top levels of gold-bearing quartz were sliced into gravel and sand. Rivers and streams rushing down the mountain slopes carried the gravel and sand away, and along with it the gold. Surging floodwaters of spring swept this burden far downstream, dropping it when rocks or sand bars blocked the free flow of the water. So the brooks and creeks of the Sacramento Valley filled up with treasure.

Gold is eight times as heavy as gravel and sinks fast. Nuggets and flakes and particles of gold landed on the beds of the streams and worked their way out of sight, burrowing into the crannies and crevices, and in time coming to rest on the solid sheets of rock underlying the streams. Hardly any of these bits of gold, freed from the grip of mountain rock, would remain in view near the surface. Thus it was purely by luck that Jim Marshall spied gold flakes in the race of Sutter's Mill. Water pouring out of Marshall's dam into the millrace had cut away the surface soil and stones to reveal the golden bounty beneath. Before long, prospectors were standing knee-deep in every stream in California, trying to find the minute particles of gold that were scattered through the sandy beds.

Gold set free from rocks and mixed with stream bed sand and gravel is called *placer* gold. Placer mining was the only kind that was practiced in California in the first two years of the gold rush. It was brutal, back-breaking work. The prospector squatted beside a stream and dipped a "washbowl," or flat basin, into the water, scooping up a panful of dirt. Then he performed the delicate and difficult task of panning for gold by swirling the contents of the washbowl around and around. The trick was to let the surplus sand and gravel spill over the edge of the pan, while any gold that might have been scooped up stayed inside. Since the gold was much heavier than the gravel, it would settle to the bottom of the basin, where the prospector would find it, if he was lucky, after he had panned out all the useless gravel.

Placer gold hardly ever was found in large quantities. It usually occurred only as fine dust or flakes, and it took a lot of panning to collect even a few dollars' worth. Sometimes, of course, a lucky prospector came upon a large nugget. In 1850 a man found a 25-pound chunk of gold, and the next year a 28-pound nugget turned up. Then a $38,000 nugget weighing 141 pounds (with 20 pounds more of quartz attached) was found, and in 1854 the biggest lump of gold ever discovered in California, the Calaveras Nugget, which weighed 195 pounds, was valued at $43,500. These finds were the exceptions, though, and no one could depend on pulling nuggets from the streams. Patiently, doggedly, the placer miners swirled their pans around, often washing some of the gold over the sides of the pans in their carelessness, and gradually collected enough metal to make their labors worthwhile.

Panning for gold was too slow and too chancy to satisfy the dreams of most prospectors. Very early in the game, some ingenious miners rigged up a device that would do the job of panning for them, sifting vast quantities of gravel in wholesale lots. Colonel R. B. Mason, the military governor of California, described one such operation at a mining camp "twenty-five miles up the American Fork, to a point now known as the Lower Mines or Mormon Diggins," which he visited in June of 1848. In his report to President Polk two months later he declared:

The hill sides were thickly strewn with canvas tents and bush arbours; a store was erected, and several boarding shanties in operation. The day was intensely hot, yet about two hundred men were at work in the full glare of the sun, washing for gold—some with tin pans, some with close woven Indian baskets, but the greater part had a rude machine, known as the cradle.

This is on rockers, six or eight feet long, open at the foot, and at its head has a coarse grate or sieve; the bottom is rounded, with small cleets nailed across. Four men are required to work this machine; one digs the ground in the bank close by the stream; another carries it to the cradle and empties it on the grate; a third gives a violent rocking motion to the machine; whilst a fourth dashes on water from the stream itself. The sieve keeps the coarse stones from entering the cradle, the current of water washes off the earthy matter, and the gravel is gradually carried out at the foot of the machine, leaving the gold mixed with a heavy fine black sand above the first cleets.

The sand and gold mixed together are then drawn off through auger holes into a pan below, are dried in the sun, and afterwards separated by blowing off the sand. A party of four men thus employed, at the lower mines, averaged $100 a day. The Indians, and those who have nothing but pans, or willow baskets, gradually wash out the earth, and separate the gravel by hand, leaving nothing but the gold mixed with sand, which is separated in the manner before described.

These crude cradles, or rockers, began to be replaced about 1851 by more elaborate devices called "long toms." These were wooden troughs twenty to thirty feet long and about eight inches deep, which widened at one end and were floored there with a sheet of iron some six feet long. The iron was perforated with holes the size of large marbles. Beneath this section, known as the "riddle," was a second trough called a "riffle-box." Mrs. Louise Clappe, who came to California with her husband, a doctor, in 1849, published this account of a long tom in action in *The Pioneer: or California Monthly Magazine* in 1855:

It takes several persons to manage properly a long-tom. Three or four men station themselves with spades at the head of the machine, while at the foot of it stands an individual armed "wid de shovel an' de hoe." The spadesmen throw in large quantities of the precious dirt, which is washed down to the riddle by a stream of water leading into the long-tom through wooden gutters or sluices. When the soil reaches the riddle, it is kept constantly in motion by the man with the hoe. Of course, by this means, all the dirt and gold escapes through the perforations into the riffle-box below . . . . Most of the dirt washes over the sides of the riffle-box, but the gold, being so astonishingly heavy, remains safely at the bottom of it.

With so many thousands of prospectors at work with pans and cradles and long toms, the most easily reached sources of placer gold were quickly exhausted. The rich sites were worked over many times, each man catching a few grains of gold that his predecessors had overlooked, but it became ever harder to show a profit from such ventures. The next technique to evolve was the digging of "coyote holes"—shafts driven into the earth near a stream. The miners knew that the heavy gold had gradually made its way deep into the ground, sifting a little lower every time a small earthquake shook the region; by digging through the overlying gravel and soil, they would come by and by to the solid bedrock on which the gold had finally come to rest. Some of these shafts were one hundred fifty feet deep or more.

Much more profitable was "hydraulicking"—using great quantities of water to rip away the overburden of earth and reveal the gold. The hydraulickers built dams high in the hills overlooking the placer sites and rigged boxlike pipes of wood leading from the dam to the site.

When the dam's gate was opened, water under high pressure roared down the pipe and spurted through canvas nozzles. By spraying this powerful jet of water back and forth over the face of a gravel bank, the hydraulickers tore up the gravel, ripping it loose and washing it into long toms. The gold particles dropped through into riffle-boxes, and the sifted gravel was dumped farther downstream. The early hydraulic systems gave way in time to huge machines called monitors, which hurled streams of water at one hundred miles an hour through iron pipe and demolished whole hillsides. Torrents of mud and sand flowed through the sluices, yielding a rich trove of gold. In spring, the flooding waters of melting mountain snows would slice through the heaps of dumped debris, carrying it downstream and spreading it out over thousands of acres of lowland. The burden of mud reached as far west as San Francisco Bay. The farmers who had begun to settle the land between San Francisco and the mining country objected to the havoc that the hydraulickers were causing, and by 1884 a state law put an end to this kind of mining. By then, the California gold rush was long over, and the hydraulickers had turned to other sites.

The hardest kind of mining of all was quartz or lode mining—digging shafts in the main lode itself. Because of the large investment required, few free-lance prospectors could afford to tackle this sort of work. It involved tunneling into the face of a mountain wherever a "float" or outcropping of precious metal indicated a vein of gold, and extracting the ore by blasting or drilling. Then the ore had to be crushed to powder in a stamp mill, so that the gold could be separated from the worthless quartz in which it was embedded. Sometimes a dozen or more miners would go into partnership to do lode mining, but generally they lacked the cash to drive shafts and set up stamp mills, and confined their activities to placer mining. Only later, when big business moved into the mining regions, did lode mining become important in California.

In 1848, and much more actively in 1849, prospectors poured into the Mother Lode, as California's mining country along the western flank of the Sierra Nevada was called. Spreading out along some one hundred fifty miles of the Mother Lode, they first panned the streams for "color," or traces of gold, and then set up cradles or long toms wherever it seemed that the site looked promising. Since the best sites tended to be near one another, the miners clustered too, settling in little camps that could quickly grow into towns. Louise Clappe described this process in her 1855 articles in *The Pioneer:*

> Sometimes a company of these wanderers will find itself upon a bar where a few pieces of the precious metal lie scattered upon the surface of the ground. Of course they immediately prospect it, which is accomplished by panning out a few basinfuls of the soil. If it pays, they claim the spot and build their shanties. The news spreads that wonderful diggings have been dis-

covered at such a place. The monte-leaders—those worse than fiends—rush, vulture-like, upon the scene and erect a round tent, where, in gambling, drinking, swearing, and fighting, the *many* reproduce pandemonium in more than its original horror, while a *few* honestly and industriously commence digging for gold, and lo! as if a fairy's wand had been waved above the bar, a full-grown mining town hath sprung into existence.

The land belonged to no one, except perhaps the Indians, who did not count. Therefore anybody could claim mining rights on a specific site. Mrs. Clappe explains, "As there are no state laws upon the subject, each mining community is permitted to make its own. Here [Rich Bar, California] they have decided that no man may claim an area of more than forty feet square. This he stakes off, and puts a notice upon it, to the effect that he holds it for mining purposes. If he does not choose to work it immediately, he is obliged to renew the notice every ten days, for, without this precaution, any other person has a right to 'jump' it, that is, to take it from him. There are many ways of evading the above law. For instance, an individual can hold as many claims as he pleases if he keeps a man at work in each, for this workman represents the original owner. I am told, however, that the laborer himself can jump the claim of the very man who employs him, if he pleases to do so. This is seldom, if ever, done."

A great deal of earnest thought went into the writing of each mining camp's bylaws. Usually only a handful of the miners could read and write, but the others took an active and noisy part in deciding the rules by which the community was to be governed. This is a typical mining-camp constitution, drawn up by the men of Bush Creek, California, on September 4, 1854:

> *1st.* That this district shall be known as Lower Bush Creek district.
>
> *2d.* That the boundary shall be as follows: commencing at the Upper Falls, or at the lower line of Allen's claims, and running down to the falls blasted by Brush Creek Co. in 1853, including five claims in the Rock Creek adjoining, and ten claims in Miles' Ravine.
>
> *3d.* That the claims shall be sixty feet in length, and extending from bank to bank.
>
> *4th.* That any person may hold one claim by location, and as many by purchase as he may see proper.
>
> *5th.* That any person owning claims in this district can leave and vacate the same until there is sufficient water for ground-sluicing by having them recorded in the recorder's book, giving number and location of the same within ten days after this date.
>
> *6th.* That these resolutions be published in the Nevada *Journal.*

The miners fiercely defended their rights under these bylaws. In the summer of 1851 a dispute broke out between two groups of miners at Coloma, who were working the original site at Sutter's Mill. One group known as the Tunnel Company, made up of Germans, built a dam that flooded the claims of the other group.

The angry miners above the dam called a general meeting of the community at which the Germans were fined $200 and told to lower their dam within ten days. They refused to obey, and when the ten days were up the local sheriff went to the dam with a small posse of miners to tear it down. They found it guarded by one hundred fifty armed men. The sheriff retreated, coming back a little later with two hundred armed men of his own; but by then the Tunnel Company miners, seeing that they were outnumbered, had begun to lower the dam.

At Rich Bar, justice was even simpler. In the summer of 1850 a party of Americans and a group of Frenchmen arrived at the same time and staked out rival claims. Each side made menacing gestures at the other, and the situation seemed about to become ugly. Then some shrewd soul proposed that each group nominate its brawniest man for a fist fight to settle the question of who would work the claims and who would leave. A three-hour boxing match followed, and when the Frenchman lost, the Americans were left in possession of the site without dispute. The losers were consoled somewhat when they moved a short way upstream and came upon an even richer deposit of gold. The place still bears the name of French Gulch.

The Americans at the Mother Lode rarely welcomed the intrusion of foreigners. Displaying a confused mixture of patriotism and greed, they made things as difficult as possible for those who had come to California from other lands. Near the town of Jackson some French miners had staked perfectly legal claims, but when they began to haul large quantities of gold from the river it infuriated the local Americans. They accused the Frenchmen of flying their own flag instead of that of the United States, and to avenge this "insult" they drove the foreigners out and took possession of their claims. The French and German miners had a better time of it than Mexicans and other Latin Americans, though. These were discriminated against openly, forced to pay special taxes, and mocked for their swarthy skins and because they spoke a different language. If they struck a good site, they were customarily driven off. Their treatment was so bad that some of them gave up mining altogether and earned a handsome living as bandits, robbing miners on their way back to San Francisco with gold.

At the absolute bottom of the social scale were the Chinese. There were only seven Chinese in California when Jim Marshall found gold in 1848, but within four years there were 20,000 of them, and their numbers continued to grow. No mining camp was without its corps of Chinese laundrymen. The Chinese were given the dirtiest jobs, were forced to live in special camps apart from white men, and were regarded as not quite human. Many of them went into mining, but most communities passed laws restricting the activities of Chinese miners. They were permitted to mine only in sites that

had already been picked over and abandoned by whites. Even this, though, gave them a chance of getting together more money than any peasant could hope to earn in China. By the late 1850's, one miner out of four in California was Chinese. They sent money home to relatives in China, and arranged for their own bodies to be shipped to China for burial when they died. At all times they were a separate community within the mining district, following their own customs and suffering severely from persecution.

Negroes were not treated as poorly as the Chinese. Slavery was still legal in much of the United States during the gold-rush years, but there was officially no slavery in California. Many southerners brought their own slaves with them, but they became free by law once they entered the state, and continued to work for their masters only out of personal loyalty. Many of the Negroes in the mines were free men. J. D. Borthwick, a Scottish artist who had caught "California fever" while living in New York in the spring of 1851, told of the Negro miners in his book, *Three Years in California,* published in 1857:

> In the mines the Americans seemed to exhibit more tolerance of Negro blood than is usual in the States—not that Negroes were allowed to sit at table with white men, or considered to be at all on an equality, but, owing partly to the exigencies of the unsettled state of society, and partly, no doubt, to the important fact that a [Ne-

gro's] dollars were as good as any others, the Americans overcame their prejudices so far that Negroes were permitted to lose their money in the gambling rooms; and in the less frequented drinking-shops they might be seen receiving drink at the hands of white barkeepers. In a town or camp of any size there was always a "nigger boarding-house," kept, of course, by a darky, for the special accommodation of colored people; but in places where there was no such institution, or at wayside houses, when a Negro wanted accommodation, he waited till the company had finished their meal and left the table before he ventured to sit down.

Borthwick, who had traveled to California by sea, had only fair luck as a miner, but earned a good deal of money by doing sketches and portraits of the successful prospectors. The first place he settled in was the lively town of Placerville. No gold has been mined there in more than a century, and the permanent population is a fraction of what it was back then. But in Borthwick's time Placerville was one of the biggest and most venerable cities of the Mother Lode. It was all of three years old when he arrived, and already had a considerable history.

Three prospectors had discovered gold there in the summer of 1848. The stream in which they panned was so low that they named their camp Dry Diggings. When other camps with the same name sprang up elsewhere, the settlement changed its name to Old Dry Diggings. Then, as its population swelled, it adopted the more imposing label of Ravine City. During this phase of the town's existence, it attracted a great many gamblers and criminals, for lawless men always were quick to move in when plenty of newly mined gold was in circulation. In January 1849, five men entered the bedroom of a Mexican gambler named Lopez to rob him at gunpoint. Though a pistol was at his head, Lopez yelled for help, and miners rushed in to arrest the burglars. Since Ravine City lacked a sheriff, a judge, or even a jail, the problem of dealing with the criminals was complicated. At length the miners picked a temporary judge and a twelve-man jury, and began to hear the case.

The guilty five were quickly sentenced to receive thirty-nine lashes apiece. When this had been carried out, three of the five—two Frenchmen and a Chilean— were placed on trial again for robbery and attempted murder in another mining camp a few months before. The men, exhausted from their whipping, were unable to stand or to speak as the evidence was offered, and speedily they were found guilty. "What shall be done with them?" the judge asked the two hundred assembled miners. "Hang them," someone shouted. One miner climbed on a stump to beg for mercy for the condemned men, saying that the proceeding amounted to nothing more than a lynching. But his voice was drowned out by the general excitement. Nothing could stop those who wanted to make a dramatic display of law and order, Ravine City style. The three culprits were placed aboard a wagon, and ropes were tied about their necks and fastened to the bough of a tree. Then the wagon was pulled forward, leaving the criminals dangling. They were cut down later and buried in their own blankets. From this affair, Ravine City became known as Hangtown.

By the time J. D. Borthwick got there in 1851, Hangtown was formally known by the more dignified name of Placerville. But the miners still called it Hangtown, and both names were used interchangeably for a long time. One of Placerville's restaurant specialties, the "Hangtown Fry," can still be found on a few California menus. The story goes that a miner fresh from the gold-fields swaggered into the town's best hotel one day in 1849, dumped a load of gold on the counter, and asked the waiter what was the most expensive dish in the place. "Oysters," he replied, "and eggs come next." The miner said, "Fry a mess of both and throw in some bacon." That was the origin of the Hangtown Fry.

Borthwick described three-year-old Placerville as

one long straggling street of clapboard houses and log cabins, built in a hollow at the side of a creek, and sur-rounded by high and steep hills. The diggings here had been exceedingly rich—men used to pick the chunks of gold out of the crevices of the rocks in the ravines with no other tool than a bowie-knife; but these days had passed, and now the whole surface of the surrounding country showed the amount of real hard work which had been done. The beds of the numerous ravines which wrinkle the faces of the hills, the bed of the creek, and all the little flats alongside of it, were a confused mass of heaps of dirt and piles of stone lying around the innumerable holes, about six feet square and five or six feet deep, from which they had been thrown out. The original course of the creek was completely obliterated, its waters being distributed into numberless little ditches, and from them conducted into the "long toms" of the miners through canvas hoses, looking like immensely long sea-serpents . . . .

Along the whole length of the creek, as far as one could see, on the banks of the creek, in the ravines, in the middle of the principal and only street of the town, and even inside some of the houses, were parties of miners, numbering from three or four to a dozen, all hard at work, some laying into it with picks, some shoveling the dirt into the "long toms," or with long-handled shovels washing the dirt thrown in, and throwing out the stones, while others were working pumps or baling water out of the holes with buckets. There was a continual noise and clatter, as mud, dirt, stones, and water were thrown about in all directions; and the men, dressed in ragged clothes and big boots, wielding picks and shovels, and rolling big rocks about, were all working as if for their lives, going into it with a will, and a degree of energy, not usually seen among laboring men.

Strolling through the town, Borthwick was impressed by "the extent to which the ordinary comforts of life were attainable." The largest and most conspicuous buildings were the gambling houses, of which there were three or four, with bright chandeliers and glittering mirrors. There were boardinghouses where miners dined at an oilcloth-covered table on "salt pork, greasy steaks, and pickles," and also "two or three 'hotels,' where much the same sort of fare was to be had, with the extra luxuries of a table-cloth and a superior quality of knives and forks."

The street itself left a little to be desired. It

> was in many places knee-deep in mud, and was plentifully strewed with old boots, hats, and shirts, old sardine-boxes, empty tins of preserved oysters, empty bottles, worn-out pots and kettles, old ham-bones, broken picks and shovels, and other rubbish too various to particularize. Here and there, in the middle of the street, was a square hole about six feet deep, in which one miner was digging, while another was baling the water out with a bucket, and a third, sitting alongside the heap of dirt which had been dug up, was washing it in a rocker.

The stores of Placerville struck Borthwick as "curious places. There was no specialty about them—everything was to be found in them which it could be supposed that anyone could possibly want, excepting fresh beef (there was a butcher who monopolized the sale of that article.)" He wrote of the "brightly-colored tins of preserved meats and vegetables with showy labels" on the counters of the stores,

> interspersed with bottles of champagne and strangely-shaped bottles of exceedingly green pickles . . . . Goods

and provisions of every description were shoved away promiscuously all around the store, in the middle of which was invariably a small table with a bench, or some empty boxes and barrels for the miners to sit on while they played cards, spent their money in brandy and oysters, and occasionally got drunk.

Sunday was the big gambling day; miners from the whole district headed for Placerville to unload some of the gold they had acquired during the week. But even on weekdays, said Borthwick, "the street was crowded all day with miners loafing about from store to store, making their purchases and asking each other to drink, the effects of which began to be seen at an early hour in the number of drunken men, and the consequent frequency of rows and quarrels. Almost every man wore a pistol or a knife—many wore both—but they were rarely used. The liberal and prompt administration of lynch law had done a great deal towards checking the wanton and indiscriminate use of these weapons on any slight occasion." The town's one church, "a very neat wooden edifice, which belonged to some denomination of Methodists," appeared to be well attended. A newspaper, published two or three times a week, kept the inhabitants informed of events elsewhere. There was a doctor, in whose cabin Borthwick found lodgings.

Gold was found everywhere about:

in the beds and banks of the rivers, creeks, and ravines,

in the flats on the convex side of the bends of the streams, and in many of the flats and hollows high up in the mountains. The precious metal was also abstracted from the very hearts of the mountains, through tunnels drifted into them for several hundred yards; and in some places real mining was carried on in the bowels of the earth by means of shafts sunk to the depth of a couple of hundred feet.

Though nearly every kind of mining operation was to be seen around Placerville, Borthwick said, the principal diggings were surface mines. Bedrock lay four to seven feet down, and the placer gold had worked its way through the dirt to come to rest there; mining consisted of stripping away the layer of "top dirt" to reach the "pay dirt" containing the gold. ("I should mention," Borthwick added, "that 'dirt' is the word universally used in California to signify the substance dug, earth, clay, gravel, loose slate, or whatever other name would be more appropriate.")

His own mining experiences were unsensational. He joined a group of Australians who were also rooming in the doctor's cabin and went with them to work a claim two miles up the creek from Placerville. It failed to pan out, and they went prospecting again, sifting through creek sand until they spied the "color," or trace of gold. In two or three days they were working a new claim a few miles from Placerville, at a settlement called Middletown. Most of the miners here were Missourians, backwoodsmen and farmers who had come West in '49. "Their costume was always exceedingly old and greasy-looking," wrote Borthwick.

> They had none of the occasional foppery of the miner, which shows itself in brilliant red shirts, boots with flaming red tops, fancy-colored hats, silver-handled bowie-knives, and rich silk sashes. It always seemed to me that a Missourian wore the same clothes in which he had crossed the plains, and that he was keeping them to wear on his journey home again.

At Middletown Borthwick watched miners' justice at work. One group of prospectors had dug a race to turn the stream from their claim, so that they could work on the exposed bed of the stream, but unhappily this maneuver would swamp the claims of some neighboring miners. They called for a court to settle the dispute, and about a hundred miners appeared. Each side picked six jurymen. Borthwick described the scene:

> When the jury had squatted themselves all together in an exalted position on a heap of stones and dirt, one of the plaintiffs, as spokesman for his party, made a very pithy speech, calling several witnesses to prove his statements, and citing many of the laws of the diggings in support of his claims. The defendants followed in the same manner, making the most of their case; while the general public, sitting in groups on the different heaps of stones piled up between the holes with which the

ground was honeycombed, smoked their pipes and watched the proceedings.

After the plaintiff and defendant had said all they had to say about it, the jury examined the state of the ground in dispute; they then called some more witnesses to give further information, and having laid their shaggy heads together for a few minutes, they pronounced their decision; which was, that the men working on the race should be allowed six days to work out their claims before the water should be turned in upon them.

Neither side was very pleased with the verdict, but both agreed to abide by it—as well they might, since the other miners were prepared to enforce the decision. "I must say I never saw a court of justice with so little humbug about it," Borthwick commented.

He moved from claim to claim, and finally found one that "paid uncommonly well." He and his partners worked the claim for six weeks, until the dry season came and the creek ran so low that they did not have enough water to operate their long tom. By the rules of the camp, they could hold the claim without working it until the following season, but since Borthwick had had enough of mining, he sold his share to the Australians and occupied himself by sketching the miners at work. Then he returned to Placerville, where he found the cabin of his friend the doctor in an upheaval:

The ground on which some of the houses were built had turned out exceedingly rich; and thinking that he might be as lucky as his neighbors, the doctor had got a party of six miners to work the inside of his cabin on half shares. . . . In his cabin were two large holes, six feet square and about seven deep; in each of these were three miners, picking and shoveling, or washing the dirt in rockers with the water pumped out of the holes . . . . They took about a fortnight in this way to work all the floor of the cabin, and found it very rich.

After a short stay Borthwick left Placerville again to tour the American River mines. He visited the site of Marshall's historic discovery, sketched and painted until his art supplies were exhausted, and made his way back to San Francisco, where he took ship for his home in Scotland.

Meanwhile the surface gold at Placerville had virtually given out. Thousands of energetic miners had ripped up the whole ravine, burrowing under the buildings and in the streets. When the easy gold was gone, most of the miners wandered eastward toward Nevada, where a new bonanza was opening up. But Placerville did not become a ghost town immediately. It was well situated on the main road between the Mother Lode and the new Nevada mines, and it became an inland trading center for those journeying between Nevada and San Francisco. Several stagecoach companies opened offices in Placerville, as did the telegraph company and the Pony Express. Merchants and craftsmen prospered by supplying the needs of the miners bound for Nevada. Among them was a man named John M. Studebaker, who made miners' wheelbarrows until he saved enough money to go back East and found a wagon factory—which later started making automobiles.

For a good part of the year winter snows in the Sierra Nevada Mountains cut the new mining camps in Nevada off from Placerville. Neither the stagecoaches nor the Pony Express could get through, but one man could—John A. "Snowshoe" Thompson, the Placerville postman. Thompson, a Norwegian, came with his family to the United States at the age of ten, in 1837. He grew up in Illinois and Missouri, and was infected with the gold fever in 1851. His first stop was Hangtown, where he prospected for a while, but the uncertainties of a miner's life did not appeal to him, and he bought a ranch in the Sacramento Valley. Ranching, too, seemed not to be what he wanted. In the winter of 1856 he heard that the Nevada camps were cut off by high snows and the mail could not go through; and suddenly John Thompson discovered his purpose in life.

As a boy in Norway he had become expert in the use of snowshoes—not the wide Canadian type, but the Norwegian kind, which looked something like long thin sled runners. From memory he built himself a pair of snowshoes ten feet long and four inches wide. They weighed twenty-five pounds, and it took a few days of practice before he was comfortable on them. Then he went down to Placerville to demonstrate his skill. Dan de Quille, an old-time Nevada newspaperman who wrote about Snowshoe Thompson in 1886, told how,

> Mounted upon his shoes . . . and with his long balance-pole in his hands, he dashed down the sides of the mountains at such a fearful rate of speed as to cause many to characterize the performance as foolhardy. Not a few of his old friends among the miners begged him to desist, swearing roundly that he would dash his brains out against a tree or plunge over some precipice and break his neck. But Thompson only laughed at their fears. With his feet firmly braced, and his balance-pole in his hands, he flew down the mountain slopes, as much at home as the eagle soaring and circling above the neighboring peaks.

From this description it is clear that Thompson's "Norwegian snowshoes" were actually skis—the first skis ever seen in California. But to men of mining camps they were simply some newfangled kind of snowshoes, and they always referred to their builder as Snowshoe Thompson.

Snowshoe volunteered to carry the mail across the mountains. He made his first trip in January 1856: "from Placerville to Carson Valley, a distance of ninety miles," Dan de Quille reported. "With the mail bags strapped upon his back, he glided over fields of snow that were in places from thirty to fifty feet in depth, his long Norwegian shoes bearing him safely and swiftly along upon the surface of the great drifts."

To the men on both sides of the mountains he became a necessity. In winter he provided the only land communication between the eastern United States and California. And he also was the only link between the miners of Nevada and their brethren on the western side of the mountains. In the wildest storms he set out unafraid, carrying sixty or eighty pounds of mail strapped to his back. It took him three days to make the journey from Placerville to Carson Valley, but the return trip, which was downhill most of the way, took him only two. His route passed through forlorn wilderness. He carried no blankets, nor even bothered to wear a coat; exercise, he said, kept him warm. His food was a little dried sausage and a few crackers; for drink he scooped up a handful of fresh snow. He never carried brandy or whiskey or any other kind of liquor, and after the first year or two he stopped taking a gun with him, since he found no use for it.

Never did he get lost. He told Dan de Quille, tapping his forehead,

I've got something in here that keeps me right. I have found many persons who were lost—dozens of men—but I have never been lost myself. There is no danger of getting lost in a narrow range of mountains like the Sierras, if a man has his wits about him.

61

His only frightening moment in more than twenty winters of carrying the mail across the Sierras came in 1857, he told de Quille.

> I came to a place where six great wolves—big timber wolves—were at work in the snow, digging out the carcass of some animal. Now, in my childhood, in Norway, I had heard so many stories about the ferocity of wolves that I feared them more than any other wild animal. To my eyes, those before me looked to have hair on them a foot long. They were great, gaunt, shaggy fellows. My course lay near them. I knew I must show a bold front.

He skied toward them, and, as he approached

> the wolves left the carcass, and in single file came out a distance of about twenty-five yards toward my line of march. The leader of the pack then wheeled about and sat down on his haunches. When the next one came up he did the same, and so on, until all were seated in a line. They acted just like trained soldiers. I pledge you my word, I thought the devil was in them!

Expecting to have the pack dash at him at any moment, the weaponless Thompson kept as calm as possible and continued on his path, passing the file of wolves "as a general moves along in front of his soldiers." They howled menacingly at him, but they did not move. When he was well past them, he looked back and saw that they had returned to the carcass. "Had I tried to run away when they marched out to meet me," he said, "I am confident the whole pack would have been upon me in a moment. They all looked it. My *show* of courage intimidated them and kept them back."

In 1859 Thompson carried the mail to Six Mile Canyon in Nevada, where the present town of Virginia City is located. Two miners, named Peter O'Reilley and

Pat McLaughlin, had come upon a peculiar sort of ore there, a heavy blue material that contained gold but that also seemed to carry another mineral. Thompson brought a chunk of this stuff back to Placerville on his return trip and showed it to Professor W. Frank Stewart, a geologist and mining expert who was also the editor of the Placerville *Weekly Observer*. Stewart immediately identified the blue substance as silver ore of the richest kind. The news traveled swiftly, and soon the great silver rush of Nevada was on. Placerville nearly emptied out as the prospectors headed for the new bonanza.

Thompson himself continued to run his ranch in the summer and haul the mail in the winter. He kept out of the mining excitement entirely. There was almost no pay in the mail route, but he stuck to it out of pride and a sense of obligation, knowing that he alone could handle the job. In 1874, when he was forty-seven years old, he began to think that the government might reward him a little more generously for his services. He sent a petition to Washington, signed by his many friends in the mining camps, asking Congress for $6,000 in back wages for his many years of service. When nothing came of this, Thompson boarded a train at Reno, Nevada, to go to Washington. Three days after it set out, the train got stuck in a huge snowdrift in Wyoming. Men shoveled for a full day to get it loose and failed. Thompson grew impatient and left the train, marching thirty-five miles to the town of Laramie in a high gale and temperatures of fifteen to thirty degrees below zero. At Laramie he found another train that was also caught in the snow, so he walked on to Cheyenne, covering a distance of fifty-six miles in two days. There he boarded a train just starting out, and continued his journey eastward. Newspapers in the East gave much attention to his feat of having outwalked the "iron horse." He was the first man who had succeeded in getting through from the West in two weeks—and he had done it without his skis, in ordinary boots. Even so, Congress failed to provide any funds for him.

His endurance and his phenomenal physical strength made him the wonder of the region. He was modest, hard-working, and totally unafraid of hardship or danger, and when he died suddenly of a liver ailment in 1876, only forty-nine years old, he was universally mourned.

Placerville, Snowshoe Thompson's home base, continued to flourish during the years he was carrying the mail. A newspaperman named J. Ross Browne visited it in 1859, just when the big silver mines of Nevada's Washoe district were opening up, and wrote, "When I looked over the busy town, and saw the long pack-trains winding their way up the mountains, I felt proud of California and her people. There is not a prettier little town in the state than Placerville, and certainly not a better class of people anywhere than her thriving inhabitants." The town, he said, was "in commotion," for it was full of adventurers bound for Washoe.

> The gambling and drinking saloons were crammed to suffocation with customers practicing for Washoe. The clothing stores were covered with placards offering to sell goods at ruinous sacrifices to Washoe miners. The forwarding houses and express offices were overflowing with goods and packages marked for Washoe . . . . Every arrival from the mountains confirmed the glad tidings that enormous quantities of silver were being discovered daily in Washoe. Any man who wanted a fortune needed only to go over there and pick it up.

Placerville enjoyed its favored position as a halfway house between Nevada and the Pacific coast. As the Nevada mines boomed, so did Placerville; and when it was Nevada's turn to have its boom fade away, the narrow streets of Placerville no longer were thronged with hopeful prospectors. A pleasant slumber descended on Dry Diggings, alias Ravine City, alias Hangtown, alias Placerville, and today the town remains perched high in the Mother Lode country, rich with memories of its glorious past.

FOUR
Ghost Towns
of California

SCORES OF GHOST TOWNS line California's mountainous backbone. Some lie right off Highway 49, the
road that goes through the Mother Lode, but others
are harder to reach, and some are impossible to find
without the help of native guides. Most of the largest
and most interesting ghost towns of the West fall into
that last group, since the richest mine sites did not neces-
sarily happen to lie in the places where it was easiest to
build roads. Many a bustling city mushroomed in unlikely territory, clinging dizzily to some remote hillside
or nestling in a ravine that could be reached only on
muleback. These boom camps came and went before
anyone troubled to build highways in their part of the
world, and so today one often has to leave the comforts
of air-conditioned motels behind and go bouncing by
jeep over washboard roads to behold the vanished splen-
dors of some famed mining town.

Volcano, California, a short distance south of Placerville, lies east of the main highway, on an up-and-down side road. The town is set in a circular valley ringed with wooded hills, and once it was believed that this was the crater of an extinct volcano—hence the town's name. (The volcano theory was wrong.) Prospectors were at work in Volcano early in 1848—some claim that gold was discovered there even before Jim Marshall saw the yellow gleam at Sutter's Mill—and the early return was handsome. Prospectors using the slow, strenuous washbowl method panned $100 a day without real strain, and it was not unusual to clear $1,000 or more a day, or to dredge up $500 worth of gold in a single pan of pay dirt. When word of this got around, Volcano boomed. Its population swelled to eight thousand; there were five hotels, a dozen restaurants, two breweries, forty-seven saloons, a church, and a fancy jail made of steel plates set between thick planks. The culture-hungry prospectors set up a Miners' Library Association and a Thespian Society for amateur theatricals. Adams Express and Wells Fargo, the two main shipping companies, opened offices for the dispatch of gold bullion to San Francisco. In 1854, the magnificent St. George Hotel went up, three stories high and the biggest building in town.

The panning prospectors soon were replaced by hydraulickers, who went about their work so energetically that they managed to undermine the foundations of half the city. Hillsides crumbled and whole streets disappeared, so that the St. George Hotel, originally near the center of town, soon stood at the edge of what remained. Some $90,000,000 of bullion was shipped from Volcano during the 1850's. Not all of it reached the bankers of San Francisco by a direct route; highway bandits had a disturbingly regular habit of swooping down and intercepting the Wells Fargo and Adams Express stagecoaches as they left town laden with gold. This happened so often that the miners began to suspect that the express company agents were tipping off the

highwaymen, and sharing in the loot afterward. To test this notion, they shipped out some crates filled with rocks. The bandits, forewarned, left them alone, but pounced on the next gold shipment to leave. A few more experiences like that and the express companies had to close their Volcano offices for lack of customers.

Then the mine production tapered off, and Volcano joined the ranks of the ghost towns. Its population today is sparse, but a good deal of the old boom city remains: the hotel, the jail, the walls of two saloons, the Adams Express office, and many other old buildings. Behind the town rises the dreary heritage of the hydrau-licking days: upturned earth and strewn boulders.

Feeble life still flickers in Volcano, but none at all in Bodie, once famed for its robust badmen. Bodie was not a town of the true Mother Lode; it lies east of the Sierra, near Mono Lake, almost at the Nevada border. Prospectors who had failed to strike it rich on the other side of the mountains began drifting east as early as 1852, into the desolate, bleak sagebrush country. In 1857 the first real ore discovery was made there, near Mono Lake, and a settlement called Monoville sprouted. Two years later a group of miners set out from Monoville to probe the high valleys nearby. They found gold just as winter was coming on. Two of the men, E. S. Taylor and William S. Bodey, went back to Monoville with some gold dust to buy provisions for the others.

A blizzard caught them as they were returning to

the mine. Bodey did not have the strength to go on; Taylor carried him as far as he could, then had to leave him, wrapped in a blanket, while he went in search of help. When Taylor returned, there was no sign of Bodey, and it was impossible to find him in the driving snow. His corpse was not discovered until spring. By then, a small town had appeared at the mine site, and it was named Bodey in honor of the ill-fated prospector. But a sign painter thought that the name looked better spelled "Bodie," and his spelling stuck.

Bodie Bluff, as the area was called, turned out to be studded with gold. Despite the barren and forbidding nature of the countryside, miners came, some content to work the placer deposits at the surface, others driving shafts into the mountainside. All provisions had to be hauled by ox-drawn wagons from a town in Nevada forty miles away. That active traveler J. Ross Browne visited Bodie in 1864, and the following year he wrote about his journey in an article for *Harper's Monthly*.

He described Bodie Bluff as "a conical hill, surmounted by a range of ·reddish-colored cliffs, very rough, jagged and picturesque; a capital looking place for a den of robbers or a gold mine . . . . The entire hill as well as the surrounding country, is destitute of vegetation, with the exception of sage-brush and bunch grass—presenting even to the eye of a traveler . . . a wonderfully refreshing picture of desolation."

The mines were still undeveloped, but from their

locations Browne guessed that some lode underlay the area. "I descended several shafts," he wrote. "This thing of being dropped down two hundred feet into the bowels of the earth in wooden buckets, and hoisted out by blind horses attached to 'whims,' may be very amusing to read about, but I have enjoyed pleasanter modes of locomotion." The Empire Gold and Silver Mining Company of New York, he said, had bought up most of the important mines, but individual prospectors were still taking $16 to $20 a day in placer diggings. "In fact," Browne noted, "the 'color of gold,' as the miners say, can be obtained from the surface dirt taken at random from any part of the hill."

As for the town, Browne observed, its greatness was still mostly a matter of future prospects:

There are now some fourteen or twenty small frame and adobe houses erected for the use of the workmen; a boarding house is already established; lots and streets are laid out by means of stakes; new houses are springing up in every direction, and speculation in real estate is quite the fashion. It was amusing to witness the enthusiasm with which the citizens went into the business of trading in lots. Groups of speculators were constantly engaged in examining choice locations, and descanting upon the brilliant future of the embryo city . . . . Some of the city dignitaries, duly impressed with the importance of having a view of their town appear in the illuminated pages of *Harper*, paid me the compliment to

72

attach my name to the principal street; and thus, in future ages, I confidently expect my memory will be rescued from oblivion.

The process of conducting preliminary explorations and raising the capital for large-scale mining was slow. A decade passed after the visit of J. Ross Browne before any real mining was done; but by 1876 the big Standard mine was opened, and it became apparent that Bodie lay atop a zone of ore several miles long and three-quarters of a mile wide. This was no town for placer mining. Shafts went down, and the miners hauled tons of ore from the ground to be pulverized in the big stamp mills. The ore was not particularly rich; it contained only two or three ounces of gold, worth $40 to $60, for each ton of rock. But even that was enough to let the mining companies show a profit on their work.

In 1876 a speculative air still hung over the camp. Shares of stock in the main Bodie mine were being sold for twenty-five cents apiece, and platoons of men who had been unable to find their fortunes in the Mother Lode or in the silver mines of Nevada came hurrying in, hungry for the new bonanza. Saloons and hotels and gambling halls appeared overnight. All the wood had to be hauled in from great distances, since there was no timber within miles of Bodie; this made the costs of construction shoot scandalously high, and even the price of some logs for fuel was beyond the reach of most of the men. When winter came, the mines shut down. Snowdrifts twenty feet deep piled up about Bodie's ramshackle buildings. "There's nothing to do," one miner wrote, "but hang around the saloons, get drunk and fight, and lie out in the snow and die." In the spring, though, the boom began in earnest. The mines reopened, the clatter of the big mills sounded day and night, and the price of a share of mine stock jumped to $55 as rich gold deposits were found.

Bodie had 13,000 people by the end of the year, and 15,000 the year after that. The usual breweries and boardinghouses appeared, as did a church and a bank. Wooden cabins sprawled in every direction. Three newspapers were founded, and they had plenty to report, for Bodie quickly earned a reputation as one of the most lawless towns in the West. A story circulated that a child whose family was moving to Bodie from a Nevada mining town closed her prayers on the day of departure by saying, "Good-by, God, we're going to Bodie," although the *Bodie Free Press* patriotically claimed that she had really exclaimed, "Good, by God, we're going to Bodie!"

There were two cemeteries in Bodie—one for the decent folk, and one for the gamblers and gunmen. The second graveyard was the one that filled faster. A single week in 1879 saw six men shot to death in local feuds. A little later, two gun-toting miners had a little too much to drink and began to brag to each other about their marksmanship; they stepped out in back of the

saloon for a test of skill, and the next day Bodie's citizens celebrated a double funeral. Life was rough and short in Bodie, but so long as the mines kept producing, the population grew.

In 1879 the hillside grave of William S. Bodey was discovered, and the remains of the town's founding father were transferred to the Bodie cemetery, along with a gun, a necktie, a bowie knife, a shoe button, a blanket, and a cloth, all of which had been originally interred with him. The following year the good folk of Bodie conceived the idea of erecting a handsome monument over his new grave. Money was raised and a magnificent tombstone was ordered from an eastern firm. The tombstone did not arrive until the fall of 1881, and the same stagecoach that brought it also carried news of the assassination of President James Garfield. Bodie's inhabitants decided on the spot to inscribe the grand tombstone in honor of the martyred President. The towering marble obelisk still occupies the most conspicuous spot in Bodie's cemetery. Old Bill Bodey had to do without a memorial until 1957, by which time the site of his second grave had been forgotten; a horizontal granite marker was placed in the graveyard with an inscription declaring that his grave lies somewhere thereabouts.

The chief mine at Bodie produced $14,500,000 worth of gold in a quarter of a century. Most of this was taken out between 1877 and 1883. For a while the lode was yielding $400,000 of bullion a month. Then it started to become harder to work the vein; there was still plenty of gold under Bodie Bluff, but the richest concentrations had already been cleaned out. What remained was mixed with rock in such meager proportions that the cost of extracting and milling the ore was greater than the value of the gold it held.

One by one the mines began to close and the miners looked for work elsewhere. Early in the twentieth century the mine known as the Standard, which had been the best producer in Bodie's boom years, was shut down, and the mining equipment was taken out of it. By 1920 or so Bodie had only a few dozen inhabitants. Most of its houses were empty. Occasionally sightseers would drive out to the ghost town to see meals still on the tables, drinks standing untouched on the bars, billiard balls sprawling on the green felt in the pool hall tables, and schoolroom slates bearing the last lesson. Among the loyal few who would not admit that Bodie was dead was an old man named Kane, who had run the bank in Bodie during the gold days. Kane always claimed that some day the mines would reopen and the town would come back to life. So every morning for more than fifty years he opened the bank in the deserted town at ten o'clock, waited patiently all day for the depositors that did not come, and closed up at three. His faith was rewarded about 1930, when some of the old mines did open again.

Bodie's rebirth was short-lived. In June 1932, a fire swept through the town, devouring the dry wooden buildings. Mr. Kane's bank was destroyed and so were many of the old shops and saloons. Some mining was done on an on-and-off basis after that; even the great old Standard mine was reopened for a while. But the low-grade ore discouraged such efforts. By 1940 the mines of Bodie were quiet again, probably forever. The permanent population of the town in 1946 was eight; a few years later no one lived there at all. Now the merciless sun beats against the crumbling houses and the rickety wooden sidewalks, and at night the bitter mountain wind sings through the haunted streets.

In 1962 the town was designated Bodie State Historic Park, and now it has a resident supervisor who is virtually the only permanent inhabitant. The California Department of Parks and Recreation has fire-proofed all the buildings and has sprayed their foundations with a wood preservative. The idea is to maintain a state of "arrested deterioration" in which the town will not be rebuilt but will not be allowed to decay beyond its condition as of 1962. A stack of lumber sits beside the house occupied by the park supervisor and his wife; it is aging in the open air, so that it will look properly weathered in case any of the boards must be replaced in the old buildings.

Not all of the ghost towns have been left to the

mercy of the elements. A few have been preserved as museums of the boom days; the tumbledown shacks have been restored, further dilapidation has been stopped, and state authorities try to maintain the place just as it was in the good old days. Sometimes this results in a phony, offensive mood of artificial antiquity, all too plainly designed to amuse tourists and part them from their dollars. But where the restoration has been done honestly and well, it is possible briefly to feel as though one were stepping back into the lively 1850's.

Columbia, California, is one of the better restorations. Though it was never entirely abandoned, it was populated only by a few old men in 1928, when the California State Park Commission conducted a survey of state historic sites. Frederick Law Olmstead, who made the survey, pointed out that Columbia was the last of the Mother Lode mining towns to survive in a good state of preservation. Twenty or thirty of its main buildings dated from the 1850's, and the town still had a gold-rush atmosphere. Olmstead recommended that the state buy the whole town and turn it into a memorial to the spirit of the forty-niners. Seventeen years went by before anything was done; but in 1945 California did acquire Columbia and incorporate it into its state park system, thus preserving an authentic example of an old-time mining camp. Now known as Columbia Historic State Park, it has been carefully restored under the direction of historians, and thousands visit it every year.

Actually, Columbia was born late in the California gold rush. Dozens of camps preceded it in the southern part of the Mother Lode, and not until March of 1850 did anyone strike gold at its site. The story goes that a group of Mexican prospectors who had been working at Santiago Hill, a mile to the northwest, found "color" in the red earth of a pleasant glade of tall oaks. The Mexicans were careless enough to mention their good luck to a group of American prospectors, led by Dr. Thaddeus Hildreth, that passed through the area. The Americans camped there overnight and were drenched by a heavy rain. In the morning, while waiting for their gear to dry, they did a little panning in a nearby gulch and quickly collected an ounce of gold. The place looked so promising that they ran the Mexicans off their claims, claimed it themselves, and named their new camp Hildreth's Diggings.

The next day, March 28, 1850, the Hildreth party started to dig. They took out fifteen pounds of gold that day, and fifteen more the next. With gold then selling at $16 an ounce, they had struck it rich. The news traveled with the customary swiftness, and in a few days Hildreth's Diggings overflowed with miners trying to stake claims adjoining the first ones. The nearby mining town of Sonora suffered a sudden loss of population as the exodus to Hildreth's Diggings began. Within a month, five thousand men were camped in the gulch below what had come to be called Kennebec Hill. The name of the place was changed to American Camp, and then in 1851 to Columbia.

Columbia, said the Sonora *Herald* in the spring of 1851, was growing as if "touched by a magic wand." Forty saloons and gambling halls lined Main Street. Seventeen general stores, eight hotels, three churches, three theaters, two fire companies, and four banks sprang up. Streets with names like Jackson, Washington, Broadway, State, Fulton, Gold, and Silver were laid out. The Chain Lightning Express brought mail and newspapers from other towns. Eight stagecoaches a day traveled between Columbia and Sonora. A newspaper, the Columbia *Star*, began publication on October 25, 1851. A certain Mrs. Denoille, who kept a popular boardinghouse, purchased the first copy off the presses at the price of an ounce of gold dust. She had arrived in Columbia not long before—the first American woman to set foot in the place—and the enthusiastic miners had welcomed her with a brass band and a parade four miles long.

No one could keep an accurate count of Columbia's population, because the growth was so rapid. Some said it was ten thousand, some said fifteen thousand, some said thirty thousand. By November 1853, Columbia was the third largest city in California—maybe the second, behind San Francisco—and the citizens decided that it deserved to be the state capital. The capital then was at Benicia, northeast of San Francisco. A solemn petition was drawn up, requesting the State Legislature to transfer the capital to Columbia, and ten thousand Columbians signed it. Pending the appointment of a committee to take the petition before the legislators, the document was stored in a Columbia bank vault.

While this was going on, a certain Peter Nicholas of Saw Mill Flat quarreled with one John Parrot of Pine Log in a Columbia store and stabbed him to death. Nicholas was instantly seized by a band of miners who hustled him off to a gulch back of the Broadway Hotel and set about the job of hanging him. They strung Nicholas to a tree, but the limb cracked under his weight. Moving him to another tree, they were about to try again when the sheriff finally arrived, broke up the lynch mob, and took Nicholas off to jail. A few days later he was tried and sentenced to death despite the eloquent efforts of his lawyer, Horace Bull.

As the time for Nicholas' execution neared, Bull slipped into the bank and contrived to get hold of the petition to the legislature. He cut off the part about shifting the state capital and pasted on his own petition —asking the governor to spare Peter Nicholas. When the petition got to Benicia, Governor John Bigler decided that this Nicholas must be a worthy and important figure, and without knowing anything about the case, canceled his death sentence. Nicholas served four years in prison, then was released; and Columbia never became the capital of California. (With the exception of a single day. When Governor Earl Warren came to Columbia on July 15, 1945, to declare the town a Historic State Park, he proclaimed it California's capital for the day, and signed official documents in a "governor's office" in the town barber shop.)

All through 1853, 1854, and 1855, a steady flow of gold streamed out of Columbia. Wells Fargo shipped $100,000 worth a week. Most of it was gold dust that miners had painstakingly sifted from the dirt, a flake or two at a time. Such men earned only about $20 a day, but even that was more than most people made in several weeks back East. Some lucky ones hit big nuggets. A man named John Stone, who played the guitar in a Columbia saloon and was famous for his song, "Hangtown Gals," dug out a single nugget worth $15,000 in 1853. He took off for San Francisco at once, sold his gold to the mint, and proceeded to squander his fortune in riotous living. When the money was all gone, he went back to playing guitar in saloons, and eventually committed suicide. Another big winner was Charles Jarvis, who in 1855 came upon a 132-pound nugget in Columbia's Poverty Gulch. He cleared $28,000 from it, lived the life of a millionaire for a year, and was killed in a barroom brawl.

The town's big problem was its water supply. There was not enough water for drinking and not nearly enough for mining. The men could get along without drinking water—one Charles Bassett fattened his bank account by peddling milk to the miners at "one dollar a whiskey bottle full"—and the lack of bathing facilities upset nobody. But water for mining was vital. There was plenty of placer gold to be mined, but the only streams in the vicinity were scanty and undependable. Without abundant water, it was impossible to run the cradles and long toms that separated the gold from the dirt. The first miners at Columbia were forced to load dirt into sacks, haul it a long way to one of the few streams, and sluice water through it to free the gold—a slow, exhausting business at best. When dry weather came, even these streams vanished, and mining operations had to halt.

A few enterprising miners drilled holes in pine poles and constructed a line of wooden pipes, bound end to end with iron bands, which brought in some water from neighboring Matelot Gulch. By 1852 the Tuolumne Water Company had been organized and was supplying water from pipes that ran many miles to town from distant Five Mile Creek. The rates of this company were shamelessly high, but it ignored the pleas of the miners to lower the charges. Like any monopoly, it tried to get all that the traffic would bear. If you needed water, you had to buy it from the company, and without water you could not mine. This state of affairs lasted until 1855, when a rival water company was finally established. The Columbia and Stanislaus River Water Company offered to sell water at half the Tuolumne Company's price—provided the miners would volunteer to help construct forty-four miles of canals and pipes.

The miners agreed. Two hundred of them, using their own tools, began to dig the Miners' Ditch on March 19, 1855. The old water company, seeing its monopoly threatened, hastily offered to cut its rates, but the miners paid no attention. They dug all day long, and when night fell the town celebrated. Tables made of planks and sawhorses were set up along the length of Washington Street, bearing free food and whiskey for the heroic ditch diggers. Restaurants and hotels invited anyone and everyone to enter and help themselves, declaring that they would "serve whoever might enter without money and without price." The new water company's pipeline was soon finished, and the high price of water was never an issue in Columbia again.

A steady water supply did not keep the town safe from devastating fires. The first big one struck in 1854 when Columbia had fifteen thousand inhabitants. It did $500,000 worth of damage, and wiped out most of the downtown business district. The next day, thirty new buildings were under construction—most of them flimsy wooden firetraps just like the old ones, although some of the new buildings were built of brick or adobe —and the streets were widened to prevent a second disaster.

Disaster came anyway on a hot afternoon in August 1857. The new bell of St. Anne's Church pealed the alarm, and miners left their claims to sprint from the meadow into the town. Flames were dancing across the roof of a Chinese laundry and licking the wooden wall of the warehouse next door. Columbia's two fire companies swung into action. Fire Company Number 1 was an exclusive group that admitted only native-born Americans. It had a splendid fire engine that had been built for King Kamehameha III of Hawaii in 1850 and shipped around Cape Horn from Boston to San Francisco. The Hawaiians never appeared to pick it up, and the Columbia firemen were able to buy it at a bargain rate. While the men of Fire Company Number 1 toiled over their hand-pumped engine, Fire Company Number 2, which admitted French, Irish, and Germans, put its own pumper to work, and jets of water shot from the buffalo-hide hoses. Local Indians who had been holding a powwow in the hills came down to help. But the streams were at a summer low, and the storage cisterns soon were exhausted. The fire blazed on, while bucket brigades desperately carried water from miners' ditches, and even poured barrels of vinegar on the flames.

About midnight the blaze reached a hardware store and touched off forty kegs of blasting powder. Five men were killed, and burning timber sprayed the town. Sixteen brick houses, thought to be fireproof, were set ablaze. By morning half the town was in ruins, and in a desperate measure the Tuolumne Water Company opened its ditches, flooding the town to douse the flames. As before, reconstruction work started immediately. The Columbia *Gazette* reported in late September that "The new brick buildings in their gradual rise are a distinctive and ornamental feature of Main Street. Washington Street and the lower part of Broadway are rapidly resuming their former appearance only with new and improved costume. State Street, between Main and Broadway, will be more improved by an additional number of buildings than any part of the town destroyed by fire . . . ."

The *Weekly Columbian* issued an optimistic editorial:

In truth, Columbia now presents as many attractive features as any mining town to be met with in the mines, either north or south. It is located in a valley, with ground in abundance not only for business lots but for family residences; and right well have some of these business lots been improved; neat residences have been erected; the gardens, horticultural and vegetable, in several, the peach, pear, and apple tree may be seen growing very finely. . . .

The diggings around Columbia are deep, and from appearances, one would judge cannot be exhausted for years. Claims have been worked for years, and pay equally as rich now as when first opened. Some of them in Columbia Gulch have been sunk sixty and seventy feet without reaching bedrock, the dirt paying all the way down, and how much lower it will pay is not known.

But the frenzied boom days of Columbia were over by the mid-1850's. The mines were still producing steadily, but all the worthwhile sites had been claimed, and no new prospectors were arriving. Population stabilized at about five thousand—the hard core of permanent residents remaining after the floating population of footloose prospectors had drifted off to the latest boom camps. One of the most beloved of the permanent residents was Madame Louie, a little old French lady who took in laundry, washing and ironing the miners' shirts for seventy-five cents apiece. She raised roses in her front yard, and each day took a bouquet to Long Tom's Bar, where she was paid $2.50 for the flowers.

One of Madame Louie's countrymen, a foul-tempered old prospector who spoke only French, was accused of stealing gold from the other miners. They surrounded him, put a rope around his neck, tied it to a branch, and asked him if he had anything to say in his own defense. Since he had no way of making his thoughts known to them, he simply scowled, whereupon the miners got ready to hoist him to his death.

Suddenly Madame Louie, fat and wheezing, came wad-dling up the hill. "Stop!" she yelled. "He didn't do it! He didn't do it!"

Since she had no new evidence to offer, the hangman tugged on the rope and the old Frenchman's heels left the ground. Madame Louie let out a shrill scream, grabbed a pick from a miner, sent the hangman fleeing, and cut the Frenchman down. The miners strung him up a second time, and a second time Madame Louie charged them and let him down. This went on most of the afternoon, until the neck of Madame Louie's coun-tryman was considerably stretched; but finally, in ad-miration of the old lady's persistence, the miners agreed to forget about the lynching. Madame Louie sent her friend off to another town to have his sore neck ban-daged. A short time later, it was discovered that the real thief was a young Irishman who had put the blame falsely on the French miner. A committee of Columbi-ans spent a great deal of time tracking him all over the Mother Lode before he was caught and hanged.

The big gambler of Columbia was Nate Arnold. He had no wish to soil his hands by mining, but he was always ready for a friendly game of cards with the men returning from the diggings. One night, heading back to his cabin, Nate tripped over a rock, glared angrily at it, and discovered that he was peering at a gigantic nugget of gold. He staked a claim and had a local as-sayer, or professional mining expert, check the ore. It proved to be so good that when Nate got the assayer's report he hired a brass band and gave a one-man parade. In a short amount of time he pulled $80,000 from his mine. He got into the habit of marching into Long Tom's Bar and paying for drinks with $20 gold pieces. He never asked for change. That was his standard price for a drink.

Nate bought a fancy horse and a harness with gold trappings, and had a buggy with red wheels made for him; he married a pretty Mexican girl, and had an ugly bull-dog shipped out at great expense from the East. For a while he lived in fine style. Then his gold mine played out; his horse and his bulldog disappeared; and his back-log of $20 gold pieces dwindled to none. When he was down to his last seventy-five cents, his wife sent him to the market for meat. Instead he came back with a live owl that he had bought from an Indian. It was a cute little owl, he said, and he had always wanted an owl for a pet. Not long afterward they found Nate Arnold dead in the gulch—probably from starvation. None of the bartenders who had sold him drinks at such fancy prices cared to contribute money to give Nate the elegant funeral he would have wanted.

Columbia began to call herself the Gem of the South-ern Mines. Handsome hotels, restaurants, and office buildings were erected. The two fire companies, which functioned as social organizations when they were not fighting conflagrations, staged lavish entertainments, such as the one put on by Company Number 2 on December 3, 1860, which featured "a most beautiful supper saturated with champagne" and a concert of operatic arias sung by a visiting tenor. The Tuolumne Water Company and its younger competitor kept the water flowing into the miners' long toms, and the scales in the Wells Fargo and Adams Express offices weighed out millions of dollars in gold dust. The gamblers were busy, and so were the gunmen. The epitaphs in Columbia's cemetery tell tales of hot quarrels and tragic duels. One declares:

Joel A. Cumback, formerly of Chester, N.J.
Died June 5, 1857
Erected by his friend, Jacob R. Giddis.

And the one beside it says simply:

Jacob R. Giddis, murdered June 28, 1861.

But Columbia too was dying, and took a long time to realize it. After 1856, placer mining ceased to be profitable, and the hydraulickers moved in. Their big hoses blasted away acres of earth, and when the other miners had packed up and gone, the hydraulickers continued to ravage the ever more desolate valley. About 1863, a traveler wrote, "The gold has been mostly washed out; many miners have left, so many houses are empty of inhabitants. Many of the houses are embowered with climbing roses, now in full bloom, and the place is lovely." The loveliness did not last, for the hydraulickers moved right into the town itself, demolishing the empty houses and hosing away the ground where they had stood. Nothing was sacred to them, not even the church ground on Kennebec Hill. The big hydraulic machines got closer and closer to the graveyard, until they were right at its borders. A jet of high-pressure water sliced into the earth and exposed a leaden coffin. The miners, hushed and frightened, gathered round and looked within to discover the perfectly preserved, richly dressed body of a lovely young woman. They put the coffin's lid in place, restored the casket to the earth, and moved their hoses to another part of the valley.

Then came a time when it no longer paid to look for gold around Columbia. The cost of operations was too high. All that kept Columbia alive were the marble quarries that had come to light not far from town. A few dozen men became marble cutters. A few families stayed on to raise fruit or livestock. The town slipped into the eerie tranquility of living death. There was talk of strange organ music coming from the abandoned church late at night, or of mysterious wraiths flitting about the cemetery. Though Columbia lay only two miles off Highway 49, few visitors came.

During the Great Depression of the 1930's, when jobs were so hard to find, a few prospectors again got to work near Columbia. They took out enough gold to pay for food and lodgings, with perhaps $100 a year left over, and that was sufficient. An old carpenter named Fritz was typical of this group. A visitor once asked him how a carpenter managed to make a living in a town where no new houses had been built since about 1865.

"Come," he whispered. "I show you."

He took the visitor into the cellar of his ramshackle house. Behind the gas meter he had a private gold mine. He was taking out about $40 a month.

After Columbia became Columbia Historic State Park in 1945, a measure of life returned. The nucleus of the old town was polished up and made presentable again, so that it looked much as it had in the glory days. The two fires of 1854 and 1857 had wiped out most of the original Columbia, and the hydraulicking vandals of the early 1860's had destroyed much of what had replaced it, but a good deal remained. The Stage Drivers' Retreat, a popular saloon when it was built in 1854, was turned into a museum housing such curiosities as a share of stock in the Tuolumne Water Company and the records of the mining claims. The printing office where the Columbia *Gazette* was published was in good shape, as was the firehouse where the famous Hawaiian fire engine was stored. In 1948, when California celebrated the hundredth anniversary of the discovery of gold at Sutter's Mill, the fire engine was trundled forth, still in working order, and sent streams of water hundreds of feet down State Street. The ghosts of Columbia had plenty of company that hectic week, and today the old town, with its art galleries, its museums, its souvenir shops, and its parking lots, plays host to vast throngs of strangers who wander its faded streets in search of yesteryear.

FIVE

The Boom Moves Inland

THERE WAS PLENTY OF GOLD in the western slopes of the Sierra Nevada, but not enough to make every prospector a millionaire. A few lucky ones found the bonanza of their dreams; most of the miners scraped out not much more than a decent living, and many found nothing at all worth mentioning. Even those who pulled gold aplenty from the streams and hillsides saw much of their take eaten up by the fantastic cost of living in an area where too much money chased too little food. And there were always the squanderers who put nothing aside, like Nate Arnold, swapping gold dust for bulldogs and fancy carriages in the pleasant hope that there would always be more gold where the last batch came from.

By and by the placer gold grew harder to find along the Mother Lode. The easy pickings were gone. Big corporations had moved in to buy up the best claims, and it was hard to make a living as a free-lance prospector. Some of the old forty-niners signed up as mine hands, working for the big companies at so much per hour to haul ore from the shafts and put it through the giant stamp mills. Others gave up the mining life altogether and became farmers or ranchers. But there were thousands, hopelessly infected with the gold fever, who strapped their belongings onto the backs of mules, took their washing pans in hand, and set out in all directions to look for virgin streams.

Some went north into the hills and valleys of Oregon and Washington, following exciting rumors. When these rumors turned out to be highly exaggerated, they kept on going into Canada; in 1858 there was a major gold rush on the Fraser River of British Columbia, but the early abundance of gold failed to last. The thwarted prospectors swung back into Idaho, where some had good fortune, and in the course of a decade the wanderers crept eastward to Montana and the Dakotas.

Others followed the golden lure into Colorado, which had a stampede of prospectors in 1858 and 1859. There had long been rumors of gold in the Rocky Mountains, and when William Green Russell, a miner from Georgia, actually found some of the yellow stuff in the vicinity of present-day Denver, a frantic gold rush began, as hordes of "fifty-niners" rushed out from the eastern states under the slogan, "Pike's Peak or Bust!"

But the most spectacular of the new mining booms took place just over the Sierra Nevada from the Mother Lode, in what is now the state of Nevada. This was a natural development, since men had been drifting eastward from the Mother Lode camps since the early 1850's. Such places as Monoville and Bodie, though they lay on the California side of the boundary, were among the first of the eastern camps, and it was not long before the boom reached into the western part of the Utah Territory, which then included present-day Nevada.

The first discoveries of gold there came in 1849. The Mormons, who had built the city of Salt Lake in Utah to avoid religious persecution back East, were trying to expand their empire into California, and sent emigrants across the Sierra Navada Mountains. On their way they panned a little gold in a gulch of Carson Valley, east of the mountains. Another group mined there in 1850 and named the gulch Gold Canyon. A year later, about a hundred men from Placerville worked in Gold Canyon, but the ore was unsatisfactory—the gold was too thoroughly mixed with silver. Since an ounce of gold was then worth roughly twenty times as much as an ounce of silver, the miners regarded the silver as nothing more than a contamination of good ore.

Still, Gold Canyon did not lack for hopeful prospectors. They kept coming to explore the canyon and its neighbors in what was known as the Washoe country. Among them were two brothers, Allen and Hosea Grosch, who reached Washoe in 1853 and three years later found a deposit of "blue dirt"—silver ore. They recognized it for what it was: "quartz rotten with silver," but they kept its whereabouts a secret. Even a silver mine, they knew, could be highly profitable if the silver was found in heavy concentrations. But in 1857 Hosea Grosch cut his foot with a pick, and died of blood poisoning. About the same time his brother Allen was caught in a Sierra blizzard and suffered fatal frostbite. The secret of the silver mine almost died with them.

A local character named Henry T. P. Comstock had watched the secretive activities of the Grosch brothers with great interest. He knew they were on to something big, though he did not know what or where, and after they died he sniffed around Gold Canyon and nearby Six Mile Canyon looking for their outcropping of "blue dirt." Though he posted claims here and there, he failed to find it, and concentrated on working his own gold mine in Gold Canyon.

Meanwhile two Irish prospectors, Peter O'Reilley and Pat McLaughlin, having had bad luck in Gold Canyon, moved on to Six Mile Canyon. There they found that all the best sites had already been claimed, so they picked out a location five hundred yards up the hillside from the others and staked their claim. From a ledge of dark quartz they pulled the peculiar blue ore that the Grosch brothers had discovered. Unsure of the stuff, they sent a sample for analysis to Placerville, via the Sierra mailman, Snowshoe Thompson. In Placerville, the assayer showed that the Irishmen had come upon a rich deposit of silver ore.

Toward evening of the day they had found the dark ledge, old Henry Comstock was out on the mountain hunting for a pony that had wandered away. He found the pony, mounted him and, with his long legs dragging through the sagebrush, rode along the slope to see what might be going on. Shortly he came to O'Reilley and McLaughlin, who were putting the day's last load of pay dirt through their rockers. Comstock peered at the ore. He did not need an assayer's report to tell him that here was something unusual. He realized at once that the Irishmen had rediscovered the lost mine of the Grosch brothers, and that this was the "blue dirt" that held such promise of wealth. Calmly Comstock informed them that he owned the land on which they were working, and that the water they were using in mining came from a spring that was also his property.

It was a bald lie, but O'Reilley and McLaughlin were too flabbergasted to protest. They agreed to cut Comstock and one of his friends in on a share of their claim. Before long, the assayer's report came from California, and with it came a few sharpshooting Californians planning to get in on the bonanza.

The assayer himself, Melville Atwood, was among

them. His figures showed that the ore from Six Mile Canyon would yield $4,791 a ton in silver and $3,196 a ton in gold. Most ores were considered good grade if it was possible to get a few hundred dollars' worth of gold *or* silver out of a ton of rock. Atwood meant to buy himself a piece of the Six Mile Canyon claim. With him came Judge James Walsh, who had large mining interests in California, and a tall young man named George Hearst, who owned some mines around Nevada City, California.

They liked what they saw and quickly bought out the discoverers. Hearst picked up the claims of O'Reilley and McLaughlin for $3,500. Walsh found the fast-talking Comstock a harder man to bargain with, and had to pay him $11,000. Those were not bad prices at all for a mine that would yield millions shortly. Hearst also purchased a half interest in another newly discovered mine, the Gould and Curry, from Alvah Gould, a miner who congratulated himself for having "swindled" the Californian. Hearst paid $450 for his half-share of the Gould and Curry. The two mines together made him a multimillionaire and one of the most powerful men in the West; Alvah Gould ended his days running a peanut stand in Reno. Comstock, O'Reilley, and McLaughlin also died poor. About the only reward Comstock got was his name on everyone's lips, for the fabulous vein of silver underlying Six Mile Canyon became known as the Comstock Lode. That immortality was

probably more than he deserved, considering the shaki-
ness of his claim to the mine in the first place.

By the summer of 1859, Hearst and Judge Walsh had
developed their mines in Six Mile Canyon and were
shipping ore by muleback over the Sierra Nevada to

San Francisco, where the ore was turned into neat ingots of silver for eventual coinage as silver dollars. The year 1859 had not been a good year for the placer miners of the Mother Lode; not only was gold getting much harder to find, but it had been a summer of drought, and the hydraulickers and the long-tom operators had been forced to suspend work for lack of water. When news came that ore assaying several thousand dollars a ton had been discovered in the Washoe country, the mining camps of California experienced a sudden and violent exodus. Thousands of miners poured into Placerville, the gateway to Washoe, and outfitted themselves for the trip across the mountains.

J. Ross Browne, newspaperman and part-time government official, was a witness to this wholesale emigration. Browne's travels had brought him to Placerville in 1859, and his article, "A Peep at Washoe," published in *Harper's Monthly Magazine* for December 1860, gave this picture of the Nevada silver rush:

> An almost continuous string of Washoeites stretched "like a great snake dragging its slow length along" as far as the eye could reach. In the course of this day's tramp we passed parties of every description and color: Irishmen, wheeling their blankets, provisions, and mining implements on wheel-barrows; American, French, and German foot-passengers, leading heavily-laden horses, or carrying their packs on their backs, and their picks and shovels slung across their shoulders; Mexicans, driving long trains of pack-mules, and swearing fearfully,

as usual, to keep them in order; dapper-looking gentle-men, apparently from San Francisco, mounted on fancy horses; women, in men's clothes, mounted on mules or burros; Pike County [Missouri] specimens, seated on piles of furniture and goods in great lumbering wagons; whisky-peddlers, with their bar-fixtures and whisky on muleback, stopping now and then to quench the thirst of the toiling multitude; organ-grinders, carrying their organs; drovers, riding, raving, and tearing away fran-tically through the brush after droves of self-willed cattle designed for the shambles; in short, every imagin-able class, and every possible species of industry, was represented in this moving pageant. It was a striking and impressive spectacle to see, in full competition with youth and strength, the most pitiable specimens of age and decay—white-haired old men, gasping for breath as they dragged their palsied limbs after them in the exciting race of avarice; cripples and hunchbacks; even sick men from their beds—all stark mad for silver.

But even the biggest bonanza does not guarantee easy money for all. Mining is *work*—tough, exhausting work —and as J. Ross Browne and his companions journeyed toward Washoe, they were treated to a somber lesson in the realities of mining. "A counter-current opposed our progress," he wrote, "in the shape of saddle-trains without riders, long lines of pack-mules laden with sil-ver ore, scattering parties of weather-beaten and foot-sore pedestrians, bearing their hard experience in their faces, and solitary stragglers, of all ages and degrees, mounted on skeleton horses, or toiling wearily homeward on foot—some merry, some sad, some eagerly intent on further speculation, but all bearing the unmistakable impress of Washoe."

One hundred and fifty miners a day were entering Washoe by the fall of 1859, and clusters of tents and shanties were springing up in every canyon. The thickest concentration of settlers was forming along the eastern slope of Mount Davidson, where Six Mile Canyon and the Comstock Lode lay. A camp that Henry Comstock named Silver City took shape there. But the name did not last long. One of the most colorful of the Six Mile Canyon prospectors rechristened the camp one dark night in 1860. He was James Fennimore, a native of Virginia who had been mining without much luck in Washoe since 1851. The locals nicknamed him "Old Virginny" because he was so proud of his home state. "Old Virginny" was a whiskey-soaked character who had owned a tiny share in the Comstock Lode, but Comstock had swindled him out of it, buying his claim for a half-blind old horse. Stumbling through the canyon in the dark with a whiskey bottle in his hand, "Old Virginny" tripped and fell. The bottle smashed and the liquor went spilling across the ground. He stared mournfully for a moment and decided to make a ceremony out of it. "I christen this ground Virginia," he announced.

The name caught on. And so Virginia City came into

being—once the liveliest boom town of old Nevada, and now one of the healthiest ghost towns of the West.

It was not much of a place to begin with. Relatively few miners got to Six Mile Canyon in the fall of 1859 before the winter snows cut off transportation, and when the real multitude of prospectors showed up the following spring they found a dismal collection of hovels awash in the mud and thawing snow. "Imagine a flood in hell, succeeded by a snowstorm," one traveler said. Another vivid account came from the pen of J. Ross Browne:

> On a slope of mountains speckled with snow, sage-bushes, and mounds of upturned earth, without any apparent beginning or end, congruity or regard for the eternal fitness of things, lay outspread the wondrous city of Virginia.
>
> Frame shanties, pitched together as if by accident; tents of canvas, of blankets, of brush, of potato-sacks and old shirts, with empty whisky-barrels for chimneys; smoky hovels of mud and stone; coyote holes in the mountain side forcibly seized and held by men; pits and shafts with smoke issuing from every crevice; piles of goods and rubbish on craggy points, in the hollows, on the rocks, in the mud, in the snow, everywhere, scattered broadcast in pell-mell confusion, as if the clouds had suddenly burst overhead and rained down the dregs of all the flimsy, rickety, filthy little hovels and rubbish of merchandise that had ever undergone the process of

evaporation from the earth since the days of Noah. The intervals of space, which may or may not have been streets, were dotted over with human beings of such sort, variety, and numbers, that the famous ant-hills of Africa were as nothing in the comparison. To say that they were rough, muddy, unkempt, and unwashed would be but faintly expressive of their actual appearance; they were all this by reason of their exposure to the weather; but they seemed to have caught the very diabolical tint and grime of the whole place. Here and there, to be sure, a San Francisco dandy of the "boiled-shirt" and "stove-pipe" pattern loomed up in proud consciousness of the triumphs of art under adverse circumstances, but they were merely peacocks in the barn-yard.

Browne found very little mining going on, but a great deal of talk of future bonanzas. Sections of mines were being offered at so much per foot.

Groups of keen speculators were huddled around the corners in earnest consultation about the rise and fall of stocks; rough customers, with red and blue flannel shirts, were straggling in from the Flowery Diggings, the desert, and other rich points, with specimens of croppings in their hands, or offering bargains in the "Rogers," the "Lady Bryant," the "Mammoth," the "Woolly Horse," and Heaven knows how many other valuable leads. [Meanwhile] the wind blew in terrific gusts from the four quarters of the compass, tearing away signs, capsizing tents, scattering the grit from the gravel-banks with blinding force in everybody's eyes, and sweeping furiously around every crook and corner in search of

some sinner to smite. Never was such a wind as this—
so scathing, so searching, so given to penetrate the very
core of suffering humanity.

A San Francisco author named Frank Soulé said of
Virginia City in its infancy, "I have been through one
hundred degrees of latitude, north and south, but never
before have found so inhospitable, miserable, God-for-
saken a spot as this . . . ." J. Ross Browne agreed:
"Nothing on earth could aspire to competition with
such a place. It was essentially infernal in every aspect."
The chief hotel's floors "were covered from the attic
to the solid earth—three hundred human beings in a
tinder-box not bigger than a first-class hen-coop!" Murderers and thieves and madmen stalked through the
throngs without arousing curiosity or fear. Browne
shocked his refined eastern readers with lurid tales of
"the roaring, raving drunkards at the barrooms, swilling
fiery liquids from morning till night; the flaring and
flaunting gambling saloons, filled with desperadoes of
the vilest sort; the mad speculations and feverish thirst
for gain."

The town went berserk over silver in the spring of
1860. Only one man in fifty was mining; the others
were buying and selling shares in the mines. "Nobody
had any money," said Browne, "yet everybody was a
millionaire in silver claims. Nobody had any credit, yet
everybody bought thousands of feet of glittering ore
. . . . All was silver under ground, and deeds and mort-

gages on top; silver, silver everywhere, but scarce a dollar in coin." He told of

> crazy-looking wretches, running hither and thither with hammers and stones in their hands, calling one another aside, hurrying to the assay offices, pulling out papers, exchanging mysterious signals—who and what are all these? Oh, these are Washoe millionaires. They are deep in "outside claims." The little fragments of rock they carry in their hands are "croppings" and "indications" from the "Wake-Up-Jake," "Root-Hog-or-Die," "Wild Cat," "Grizzly-Hill," "Dry-Up," "Lame Horse," "Let-Her-Rip," "You Bet," "Gouge-Eye," and other famous ledges and companies, in which they own some thousands of feet . . . . All night long these dreadful noises continue; the ears are distracted with an unintelligible jargon of "croppings," "ledges," "lodes," "leads," "indications," "feet," and "strikes". . . .

As the shafts sank deeper into the mountain, the rich promise of the Comstock Lode was fulfilled, and shares in one claim after another soared sky-high on Virginia City's outdoor stock exchanges. The main lode ran lengthwise along the face of the mountain, and each mine owner tunneled inward at right angles to reach it, while those who preferred to play the stock market hurried to buy shares in the best mines. There were four thousand claims in Washoe by the end of 1860, but only three hundred of them had been opened, and only about twenty of these were regarded as sound investments. Most of these producing mines were controlled by George Hearst. Judge Walsh sold out too early, making a fortune but not the mighty fortune he could have had. And such dazed figures as Henry Comstock and Peter O'Reilley wandered through the confusion in tragic dismay, realizing they had parted with one of history's biggest silver bonanzas for a pitiful few thousand dollars.

Silver might turn up anywhere. J. Ross Browne describes how a man digging the foundations of a new house brought up silver ore in the middle of Virginia City:

> He immediately laid claim to a whole street covered with houses. The excitement produced by this "streak of luck" was perfectly frantic. Hundreds went to work grubbing up the ground under their own and their neighbors' tents, and it was not long before the whole city seemed in a fair way of being undermined. The famous Winn, as I was told, struck the richest lead of all directly under his restaurant, and was next day considered worth a million of dollars.

It was not necessary to own a piece of land in order to claim mining rights on it. As Browne told it:

> Owners of lots protested in vain. The mining laws were paramount where there was no law at all. There was no security to personal property, or even to persons. He who turned in to sleep at night might find himself in a pit of silver by morning. At least it was thus when I made up my mind to escape from that delectable region;

and now, four months later, I really don't know whether the great city of Virginia is still in existence, or whether the inhabitants have not found a "deeper deep, still threatening to devour."

J. Ross Browne was clearly a man with a gift for turning phrases, and if he had stayed in Virginia City a few months longer he would have enjoyed the experience of meeting a young man whose skill with the pen was at least the equal of his own: Samuel Langhorne Clemens, otherwise known as Mark Twain. Clemens was twenty-six years old, with all his literary greatness still to come, when he was drawn to Washoe by silver fever. In that year, 1861, Congress had split Utah Territory in two, creating the new Nevada Territory with its capital at Carson City. Clemens' older brother Orion received a job with the territorial government, and young Sam, whose employment as a river pilot on the Mississippi had been interrupted by the Civil War, went out to try his luck there too.

Clemens did not remain in Carson City for long. As he wrote in *Roughing It*, his autobiographical book of 1872,

"Prospecting parties" were leaving for the mountains every day, and discovering and taking possession of rich silver-bearing lodes and ledges of quartz . . . . I would have been more or less than human if I had not gone mad like the rest. Cart-loads of solid silver bricks, as large as pigs of lead, were arriving from the mills every day, and such sights as that gave substance to the wild talk about me. I succumbed and grew as frenzied as the craziest.

By then the Washoe lodes were old news; all the best claims were taken. Clemens considered going to Humboldt County, north of Washoe, or to Esmeralda County, to the south. "Every few days," he wrote, "news would come of the discovery of a brand-new mining region; immediately the papers would teem with

accounts of its richness, and away the surplus population would scamper to take possession. By the time I was fairly inoculated with the disease, 'Esmeralda' had just had a run and 'Humboldt' was beginning to shriek for attention." He picked up a copy of the *Daily Territorial Enterprise*, a newspaper published at Virginia City, and read this article:

> But what about our mines? I shall be candid with you. I shall express an honest opinion, based upon a thorough examination. Humboldt County is the richest mineral region upon God's footstool. Each mountain range is gorged with the precious ores. Humboldt is the true Golconda.
>
> The other day an assay of mere *croppings* yielded exceeding *four thousand dollars to the ton.* A week or two ago an assay of just such surface developments made returns of *seven thousand* dollars to the ton. Our mountains are full of rambling prospectors. Each day and almost every hour reveals new and more startling evidence of the profuse and intensified wealth of our favored county. . . . Have no fears of the mineral resources of Humboldt County. They are immense—incalculable.

A little research told him that the mines of the Comstock Lode were then yielding, on the average, from $100 to $400 to the ton, while these Humboldt reports indicated concentrations many times as rich. Instantly Clemens and three friends prepared to go to Humboldt —"upbraiding ourselves for not deciding sooner—for we were in terror lest all the rich mines would be found and secured before we got there, and we might have to put up with ledges that would not yield more than two or three hundred dollars a ton, maybe."

With his companions—an elderly blacksmith and two young lawyers—Clemens bought a wagon and two scrawny old horses, loaded nearly a ton of provisions and mining tools aboard, and left Carson City on a chilly December afternoon. The horses soon let it be known that they would be more comfortable if three of the men walked alongside the wagon, rather than riding in it. "But in a little while," he noted, "it was found that it would be a fine thing if the driver got out and walked also. . . . Within the hour, we found that it would not only be better, but was absolutely necessary, that we four, taking turns, two at a time, should put our hands against the end of the wagon and push it through the sand, leaving the feeble horses little to do but keep out of the way . . . ." In this manner it took fifteen days to make the two hundred-mile trip, camping in the desert and undergoing considerable hardship.

At last they came to the Humboldt mining camp named Unionville, which consisted of eleven cabins strung out in a deep canyon. "I confess, without shame," Clemens said, "that I expected to find masses of silver lying all about the ground. I expected to see it glittering in the sun on the mountain summits. I said nothing about this, for some instinct told me that I might possibly have an exaggerated idea about it, and so if I betrayed my thought I might bring derision upon myself." While the others were pitching camp, he quietly scouted around for a mine. No silver was in sight, but he was delighted to spy what surely was an outcropping of gold ore. That night he dramatically displayed a rock sample to the old blacksmith, who studied it a moment and offered an opinion: "I think it is nothing but a lot of granite rubbish and nasty glittering mica that isn't worth ten cents an acre."

Day after day they scrambled over sagebrush, rocks, and snow, burrowing here and there, breaking off fragments of rock, finally reaching a ledge of silver-bearing quartz. "We've got it!" the blacksmith cried, and held out a chunk of rock that he had split with his hammer. "The rock was clean and white, where it was broken, and across it ran a ragged thread of blue. He said that that little thread had silver in it, mixed with base metals, such as lead and antimony, and other rubbish, and that there was a speck or two of gold visible. After a great deal of effort we managed to discern some little fine yellow specks, and judged that a couple of tons of them massed together might make a gold dollar, possibly." They named their mine "Monarch of the Mountains" and the blacksmith composed a statement of claim:

NOTICE

We the undersigned claim three claims, of three hundred feet each (and one for discovery), on

this silver-bearing quartz lead or lode, extending
north and south from this notice, with all its dips,
spurs, and angles, variations and sinuosities, together with fifty feet of ground on either side
for working the same.

"We put our names to it and tried to feel that our
fortunes were made," Mark Twain wrote. But certain
practical matters remained before they could enjoy the
benefits of their wealth. The outcropping of quartz was
only a token of the ore that lay deep within the earth
at this site. How deep, no one could know without
driving a shaft. For a week they went to work with
picks, drills, crowbars, and blasting-powder. It took
a couple of hours to drill a hole two feet deep in the
rock.

We would put in a charge of powder, insert half a yard
of fuse, pour in sand and gravel and ram it down, then
light the fuse and run. When the explosion came and the
rocks and smoke shot into the air, we would go back
and find about a bushel of that hard, rebellious quartz
jolted out. Nothing more. One week of this satisfied me.
I resigned. Claggett and Oliphant followed. Our shaft
was only twelve feet deep. We decided that a tunnel
was the thing we wanted.

Another week of work produced a tunnel of modest
size. They judged that about nine hundred feet more
of it might reach their ore. "I resigned again, and the
other boys only held out one day longer. We decided

that a tunnel was not what we wanted. We wanted a ledge that was already 'developed.' There were none in the camp."

Meanwhile the region was filling up with prospectors in quest of the supposedly fabulous Humboldt mines. Clemens and his friends went into the stock-market business, picking up a few shares of this mine and a few of that in exchange for shares in "Monarch of the Mountains." Soon they owned stock in fifty-odd mines "that had never been molested by a shovel or scratched with a pick . . . . We were stark mad with excitement —drunk with happiness—smothered under mountains of prospective wealth—arrogantly compassionate toward the plodding millions who knew not our marvelous canyon—but our credit was not good at the grocer's."

Now he discovered the secret of those fantastic assay figures. They represented carefully selected samples— the richest chunks of ore. Shortly Clemens and his partners sold all their mining shares at high prices to newcomers just as enthusiastic as themselves and less well informed, and headed for other parts. After a variety of mining exploits, none of them profitable, Clemens arrived in Virginia City to take up the respectable position of city editor of the *Daily Territorial Enterprise* at a salary of $25 per week.

Virginia City was no longer the muddy, shabby collection of shacks that J. Ross Browne had mocked in

1860. The opulence of the Comstock Lode was reflected in the substantial growth of the city that rose
above it. Clinging to the steep side of Mount Davidson
at a height of 7,200 feet above sea level, Virginia City
in 1862 had a population of 15,000 or more. At any
time, half this population could be found swarming
through the streets, and the other half was at work hundreds of feet below those same streets, digging in the
tunnels leading to the Comstock Lode. The boom of
explosives could frequently be heard, and the precariously perched houses shivered with each blast.

Clemens described the scene:

> The mountainside was so steep that the entire town
> had a slant to it like a roof. Each street was a terrace, and
> from each to the next street below the descent was forty
> or fifty feet. The fronts of the houses were level with
> the street they faced, but their rear first floors were
> propped on lofty stilts; a man could stand at a rear first-
> floor window of a C Street house and look down the
> chimneys of the row of houses below him facing D Street.
> It was a laborious climb, in that thin atmosphere, to
> ascend from D to A Street, and you were panting and out
> of breath when you got there; but you could turn
> around and go down again like a house afire—so to speak.

The boom was in full swing, Clemens wrote:

> There were military companies, fire companies, brass-
> bands, banks, hotels, theaters, "hurdy-gurdy houses,"
> wide-open gambling-palaces, political pow-wows, civic
> processions, murders, inquests, riots, a whisky-mill every

fifteen steps, a Board of Aldermen, a Mayor, a City Sur-
veyor, a City Engineer, a Chief of the Fire Department,
with First, Second, and Third Assistants, a Chief of
Police, City Marshall, and a large police force, two
Boards of Mining Brokers, a dozen breweries, and half
a dozen jails and station-houses in full operation, and
some talk of building a church . . . . Large fire-proof
brick buildings were going up in the principal streets,
and the wooden suburbs were spreading out in all directions. Town lots soared up to prices that were amazing.

The original Comstock Lode ran parallel to A Street,
high on Mount Davidson. Later, a second ore zone was
opened paralleling D and E streets, and still later mines
were developed near K and L streets. Isolated mines were
worked in more remote corners of the city. Mark
Twain tells of the vast underground population of
miners that "thronged in and out among an intricate
maze of tunnels and drifts, flitting hither and thither
under a winking sparkle of lights, and over their heads
towered a vast web of interlocking timbers that held
the walls of the gutted Comstock apart. These timbers
were as large as a man's body, and the framework
stretched upward so far that no eye could pierce to its
top through the closing gloom. It was like peering up
through the clean-picked ribs and bones of some colos-
sal skeleton. Imagine such a framework two miles long,
sixty feet wide, and higher than any church spire in
America . . . ."

All the timber used to brace the shafts and tunnels

under the city had to be hauled twenty miles or more from the forests of the Sierra Nevada, since any trees in closer range had been cut in the earliest days of Virginia City. The imposing new buildings, which appeared at such a startling rate in 1861 and 1862, were also fashioned from costly long-distance timbers. But these expenses hardly mattered. Wells Fargo shipped $270,000 worth of bullion out of Virginia City in the first three months of 1862, $570,000 during the next three months, and $800,000 in the third quarter of the year. By the middle of 1863, bullion shipments had reached $500,000 *a month*.

Through this bonanza town moved Mark Twain, newspaper editor—a coatless, whiskered figure in a blue woolen shirt and rustic pantaloons stuffed into his boot-tops. In his first few days on the job he had trouble finding news and was forced to invent some. A wagon train of emigrants passed through town after having had a hard time with Indian raiders in the prairies; when the leader of the group failed to give Clemens a sufficiently detailed story of their adventures, he made up a flamboyant tale of massacre and received high praise from his publisher, who told him he was as good a reporter as Virginia City's veteran newsman Dan de Quille. "With encouragement like that," Clemens said, "I felt that I could take my pen and murder all the immigrants on the plains if need be, and the interests of the paper demanded it."

Soon, though, he learned ways to get news from the right sources. He built a network of friendships at the stamp mills, the mines, the courts, the hotels, and the police stations, and filled the columns of the *Enterprise* with his nimble journalism. He went everywhere, even into the mysterious and sinister Chinese quarter of town.

The Chinese have built their portion of the city to suit themselves; and as they keep neither carriages nor wagons, their streets are not wide enough, as a general thing, to admit of the passage of vehicles. At ten o'clock at night the Chinaman may be seen in all his glory. In every little cooped-up, dingy cavern of a hut, faint with the odor of burning Josh-lights and with nothing to see the gloom by save the sickly, guttering tallow candle, were two or three yellow, long-tailed vagabonds, coiled up on a sort of short truckle-bed, smoking opium, motionless and with their lusterless eyes turned inward from excess of satisfaction. . . .

His salary was raised to $40 a week. He watched the frenzied growth of new mine shafts everywhere, and speculated in the stock of these mines, but never took pick in hand himself; his mining days were over. "There were more mines than miners," he wrote. "True, not ten of these mines were yielding rock worth hauling to a mill, but everybody said, 'Wait till the shaft gets down where the ledge comes in solid, and then you will see!' So nobody was discouraged." The simplest way to get rich, he reported, was to "salt" a mine by purchasing some rich Comstock ore and secretly dumping it in an otherwise worthless shaft, then "discovering" the ore and selling stock in the mine at a high price. One salted mine, the North Ophir, was said to yield pure silver in small, solid lumps. Mark Twain visited it and found

a shaft six or eight feet deep, in the bottom of which was a badly shattered vein of dull, yellowish, unpromising rock .... We got out a pan of the rubbish and washed it in a puddle, and sure enough, among the sediment we found half a dozen black, bullet-looking pellets of unimpeachable "native" silver. Nobody had ever heard of such a thing before; science could not account for such a queer novelty. The stock rose to sixty-five dollars a foot .... And then it transpired that the mine had been "salted"—and not in any hackneyed way, either, but in a singularly bold, barefaced and peculiarly original and outrageous fashion. On one of the lumps of "native" silver was discovered the minted legend, "ted States Of," and then it was plainly apparent that the mine has been "salted" with melted half-dollars! The lumps thus obtained had been blackened till they resembled native silver, and were then mixed with the shattered rock in the bottom of the shaft.

In August of 1863 fire ripped through the business section of Virginia City and did $7,000,000 worth of damage. New buildings soon appeared, but in the following year a much more serious menace struck the city: the ore began to give out. The mines, which had yielded $45,000,000 in five years, closed down one by one. Samuel Bowles, a Massachusetts newspaper editor

who visited Virginia City in 1865, observed that a kind
of quiet respectability had begun to replace the naughty
gaiety of the boom years:

> It is beginning to recognize the Sabbath, has many
> churches open, and closes part of its stores on that day;
> is exceedingly well built, in large proportion with solid
> brick stores and warehouses; and though the fast and
> fascinating times of 1862-63 are over, when it held
> from fifteen to twenty thousand people, and Broadway
> and Wall street were not more crowded than its streets,
> and there are tokens that its great mines are nearly dug
> out, it still has the air of permanence and of profit, and
> contains a population of seven or eight thousand, be-
> sides the adjoining town or extension of Gold Hill,
> which has about three thousand more.

J. Ross Browne revisited Virginia City in 1865, after
an absence of four years. He wrote:

> The business part of the town has been built up with
> astonishing rapidity. In the spring of 1860 there was
> nothing of it save a few frame shanties and canvas
> tents, and one or two rough stone cabins. It now
> presents some of the distinguishing features of a metro-
> politan city. Large and substantial brick houses, three
> or four stories high, with ornamental fronts, have filled
> up most of the gaps, and many more are still in progress
> of erection.

Though mine production was dropping sharply, there
was still plenty of activity in the tunnels beneath the
city:

Perhaps there is not another spot upon the face of the globe that presents a scene so weird and desolate in its natural aspect, yet so replete with busy life, so animate with human interest. It is as if a wondrous battle raged, in which the combatants were man and earth. Myriads of swarthy, bearded, dust-covered men are piercing into the grim old mountains, ripping them open, thrusting murderous holes through their naked bodies; piling up engines to cut out their vital arteries; stamping and crushing up with infernal machines their disemboweled fragments, and holding fiendish revels amidst the chaos of destruction . . . .

Such scenes of vitality were all but unknown in Virginia City by the end of 1865. From then until 1874 the Comstock Lode was, as the miners said, *"borrasca"* —clouded over. The developed mines ceased to show a profit. Soon mortgages were being foreclosed and the Bank of California, which had financed much of the expansion of Virginia City, became the involuntary owner of many idle mines and mills. The known veins of silver had played out, and, because of hasty surveying, the huge ore bodies remaining were still undiscovered. Overlapping claims tied up much of the district in prolonged lawsuits, preventing further exploration.

Yet the ore was there, and a few shrewd men realized it. Quietly they started to buy up the "worthless" claims. These clever investors included two mine superintendents, John W. Mackay and James G. Fair, and two San Francisco saloon proprietors, James C. Flood and

William S. O'Brien. The first two provided the mining knowledge, the other two put up the cash, and they snapped up the bargains. The Hale and Norcross mine, once one of the big producers, had sold at $2,100 a share on the San Francisco stock exchange not long before; the Big Four were able to buy its stock at only $42 a share. Other mines were added to their portfolio until, by the early 1870's, they controlled the entire Comstock Lode, grouping all the mines they owned under the name of the Consolidated Virginia Mine. In March of 1873 they struck the real bonanza of the Comstock Lode—and Virginia City's boom times returned

The Consolidated Virginia bonanza dwarfed the excitement of 1859-1863. Virginia City, fueled by its gigantic lode, came back to life as one of the richest and most energetic cities of the West. The Big Bonanza began 400 feet down, and some of the mining had to be done 1,500 feet below the surface; costs ran as high as $17 per ton, but the yield was ten to twenty times as great. The new lode was more than 100 feet wide and had a value of hundreds of millions of dollars. Consolidated Virginia's stock leaped to $700 a share; the mining company was paying dividends of more than a million dollars a month; in one eight-day period its mill produced $1,110,000 in bullion. The Big Four, silver kings of the West, built lordly mansions on Virginia City's Millionaire's Row. A glittering opera house went up, and the new International Hotel, a five-story brick and stone building with gas lights and an elevator, was one of the most sumptuous in the country. Its rooms were booked for months in advance at lofty prices, and until it burned down in 1914 it was a symbol of elegance and refinement.

Mark Twain had long since gone East to win fame as a novelist, but the *Enterprise* still was published and Dan de Quille remained its star reporter. This celebrated writer of the old West, whose real name was William Wright, was born in Ohio in 1829 and arrived in California in 1857, just too late to strike it rich in the Mother Lode. He moved on into Washoe after a few years, was unsuccessful as a prospector, and found his real career when he began to write for the Virginia City *Enterprise*. He continued to contribute to the paper until its suspension in 1893; and his book, *The Big Bonanza*, published in 1876, was the first and best history of the Comstock Lode. He died in 1898.

One of Dan de Quille's most playful stories appeared in the *Enterprise* of 1874. He told of the sad fate of

Mr. Jonathan Newhouse, a man of considerable inventive genius. Mr. Newhouse had constructed what he called a "solar armor," an apparatus intended to protect the wearer from the fierce heat of the sun in crossing deserts and burning alkaline plains. The armor consisted of a long, close-fitting jacket made of common sponge and a cap or hood of the same material, both jacket and hood being about an inch in thickness. Before starting across the desert, this armor was to be saturated with water. Under the right arm was suspended an India-rubber sack filled with water and having a small gutta-percha tube leading to the top of the hood. In order to keep the armor moist, all that was necessary to be done by the traveler as he progressed over the burning sands, was to press the sack occasionally, when a small quantity of water would be forced up and thoroughly saturate the hood and the jacket below it. Thus, by the evaporation of the moisture in the armor, it was calculated might be produced any degree of cold. Mr. Newhouse went down to Death Valley, determined to try the expedient of crossing that terrible place in his armor. He started out into the valley one morning from the camp nearest its borders, telling the men at the camp, as they laced his armor on his back, that he would return in two days. The next day an Indian who could speak but a few words of English came to the camp in a great state of excitement. He made the men understand that he wanted them to follow him. At the distance of about twenty miles out into the desert the Indian pointed to a human figure seated against a rock. Approaching, they found it to be Newhouse still in his armor. He was dead and frozen stiff. His beard was covered with frost, and—though the noonday sun poured down its fiercest rays—an icicle over a foot in length hung from his nose. There he had perished miserably, because his armor had worked but too well, and because it was laced up behind where he could not reach the fastenings.

Another of Dan de Quille's tall tales involved the petrified Indian of Mono Lake, whose body had turned

completely to silver ore. Nevada readers were solemnly
told of the discovery, in a mine southeast of the lake, of a
full-grown man's body, "almost perfect, even to the
fingers and toes." As it was moved from its resting
place, an arm broke off, and one of the miners thought
of making an assay of the minerals it contained. Shortly
he announced that the petrified body was "a mass of
sulphuret of silver, slightly mixed with copper and iron
(in the shape of pyrites.)" Chemical tests showed the
presence of pure silver throughout the body. Dan de
Quille cited a great deal of archaeological and geological
evidence to show how an Indian taking refuge from a
storm in a mountain cleft might die and become miner-
alized through the action of subterranean springs.

At the height of the second Comstock boom Virginia
City was devastated once more by fire. It broke out in
Crazy Kate's lodging house on A Street one night in
October 1875, when a coal-oil lamp was tipped over
during a drunken quarrel, and quickly spread. Gideon
Anthony Hamilton, a mining engineer employed by
Consolidated Virginia, gave this description of the con-
flagration in a letter to a friend written two weeks later:

> No rain had fallen for six months. Everything was like
> tinder, and the flames leaping high into the air caught
> from side to side of the street with incredible rapidity.
> . . . Block after block of buildings went down, and the
> mighty mass of flame swept on with irresistible fury to-
> wards the great hoisting works and mill of the Ophir

and Consolidated Virginia mines .... The immense works of both mines had been finished less than a month before, and the aggregate value of their property *above ground* and occupying an area only about 300 yds square was over two millions of dollars. Besides the destruction of these works would stop the extraction of an equal value of ore *every month from the Con. Va. alone.* All hope now of saving anything between the fire and the mines was abandoned—if these could be saved it was all they could hope for; and to accomplish it, giant powder, that terrible engine of destruction, was brought into action. House after house was blown to atoms as fast as the charges could be laid. I fixed my eyes upon one palatial residence three stories high with French roof and bow windows, the property of Samuel Curtis, Supt. of the Ophir mine; and while I was wondering whether or not that would be saved, it vanished from my gaze as a soap bubble vanishes—leaving nothing but empty air where it had stood three seconds before.

The purpose of the blasting was to obliterate anything that might lead the fire to the mines by creating a great open area. But between the fire and the mines ran the railroad track, covered with cars bearing dry firewood and timbers for the shafts, and beyond these were two long wooden trestles supporting rails leading to the mill, while beside the mines themselves lay a winter's supply of firewood. "Buildings could be blown up," Hamilton wrote, "but no power on earth could instantaneously remove the great masses of material of which I have spoken." Winds of gale force hurled burning pieces of wood in a fiery shower onto the railroad track and lumberyard, which soon were ablaze.

> The heat was so intense that the chilled cast-iron car wheels melted before it just as a piece of ice melts when it is dropped upon a hot stove. The depot and freight houses came next . . . . The flames came tearing on with a front 200 yds. wide and 200 ft. high. A gust of wind from the mountain depressed them until they lapped over the whole roof of the Con. Va. hoisting works like an immense blanket. The men barely escaped with their lives, and the hoisting works and mill of the greatest mine the world ever saw . . . melted away like the "baseless fabric of a dream," leaving but holes in the ground . . . .

Finally, when there was nothing left in its path to devour, the fire died down. Thousands of homeless citizens clustered on the barren hillsides. Shares in Consolidated Virginia plunged catastrophically on the western stock exchanges. But, Hamilton wrote, "the recuperative qualities of a prosperous mining camp are something wonderful." The day after the fire construction work began in the still smoldering city. The first building to go up, predictably, was a gambling casino. Other cities sent help; the Chinese of San Francisco contributed money "to be used for all sufferers regardless of race," and scores of trains arrived every day bearing clothing, blankets, and food from the neighboring mining camps. The Virginia City that arose on the ruins was even more splendid than that which had perished.

A magnificent Catholic church rose at E and Taylor streets, displaying a bell cast from Virginia City silver. Piper's Opera House was replaced on its former site by a bigger and flashier successor. (It burned down in 1882; the present Piper's Opera House is the third of its line.) The millionaires' mansions were ever more awesome; the hotels and bars and restaurants were aglow with luxurious furnishings. A Street, the original mining sector, now became a fashionable residential district; C Street, the new business thoroughfare, blossomed with handsome brick shops and offices.

As had happened in 1862, the great fire was an omen of declining mine production. The Comstock Lode yielded $38,000,000 in 1875, but after that the dip in output was steady and severe. The mines now went so deep into the mountain that they were striking the ground water; the shafts flooded and had to be pumped at great cost. The heat underground was intense, adding to the difficulties; the water at the bottom of one mine was measured at 170° F. Men could work only fifteen minutes at a time under such conditions, and then had to spend forty-five minutes cooling off. Adolph Sutro, a San Franciscan who had been one of the early beneficiaries of the Comstock bonanza, devised a scheme as early as 1865 for driving a four-mile tunnel through Mount Davidson, two thousand feet below the surface of the mines, for drainage and ventilation. He proposed to run the water out and use it for irrigation. Sutro raised $3,000,000 for the work, despite the opposition of certain mill owners who had no wish to make mining any easier. He broke ground for his tunnel in the fall of 1869, but work was slow, and the project was not completed until July 8, 1878. Fresh air rushed through the tunnel, almost knocking the workmen off their feet as it swept away the smoke, gas, and dust that had accumulated in the labyrinth of passageways for nearly twenty years. Soon Sutro's tunnel gave him control of the Comstock, for only those mines that were linked to his drainage system could be worked. But he sold out quickly, taking a huge profit, and moved on to build a new empire in San Francisco's financial world.

Not even the Sutro Tunnel could save Virginia City. By 1881 mine output was down to $1,500,000, and the miners were drifting to other bonanzas. The Comstock Lode became only a romantic memory. Eventually the last mine was closed, never to reopen. Virginia City's population dropped below four hundred.

Its permanent population is not much greater than that today, and no mining has been done there in decades, but Virginia City is a most unghostly ghost town. The *Enterprise* has been revived and is published every week; ancient saloons such as the Washoe Club, the Crystal Bar, the Comstock House, and the Sawdust Corner still meet the needs of the thirsty; a number of the old hotels and restaurants serve the thousands of tourists who arrive each year. Such landmarks of bygone days as the spacious 1870's mansions and offices, the three surviving churches, the third Piper's Opera House, and the elegant jail are irresistible magnets for sightseers. Neither a restoration nor a reconstruction, Virginia City is an authentic relic of the bustling Comstock Lode days, kept alive by tourism now that the ore no longer comes forth from the depths of the earth.

SIX

Phantom Cities
of the Nevada Desert

THE COMSTOCK EXCITEMENT produced ripples all across Nevada's windswept, parched, barren interior. Prospectors fanned out in every direction, and as the silver frenzy rose to its dizzy peak, other mining camps appeared in unlikely corners. Nevada itself graduated from the status of a territory to that of a state in record time, entering the Union in 1864 although its total population was less than that of the city of San Francisco. (It still is. The 1960 census found only 285,000 people in all of Nevada, or not quite three to the square mile. That, however, represented a population growth of better than 150 per cent since 1940.)

Even a thriving settlement in such a sparsely populated state might pass for a ghost town elsewhere, and Nevada's true ghost towns are genuinely spooky. Among the most interesting is Austin, one hundred and sixty-five miles east of Virginia City, practically in the geographical center of the state.

Austin's boom was the result of pure luck. Pony Express riders, crossing Nevada's Reese River Valley, stopped to refresh themselves at a rest station at Jacob's Springs. Just east of the station was Pony Canyon, which led to a pass through the mountains. In May 1862, the keeper of the station was bringing a load of wood back from Pony Canyon when one of his horses kicked up a chunk of greenish quartz. The keeper picked it up, peered curiously at it for a moment, and realized that he was holding gold ore. He sent it to Virginia City for analysis, and the assayer reported that the sample contained silver as well.

Within a week ten prospectors were staking claims in Pony Canyon. By July 10, 1862, a mining district had been organized, and in the months that followed one lode after another came to light, until at the beginning of 1863 a stampede of miners began. The first arrivals settled around the station at Jacob's Springs, which became the village of Jacobsville. By March Jacobsville had declared itself the county seat and had invested the considerable sum of $8,440 in a new courthouse, which was intended as the administrative center of what had been until the previous year an uninhabited territory.

But Jacobsville was too far from the mines. A short-lived town called Clifton came into being east of the canyon, and most of Jacobsville's settlers moved there.

Almost at once a second camp, named Austin, material-
ized in Pony Canyon itself, and the inhabitants of Clifton
promptly transferred themselves to the newer and more
convenient site. In April the miners of the district met
to elect county officers and pick a permanent county
seat. Austin was chosen, and Jacobsville became an instant ghost town. By summer a road led up the canyon
to Austin, which had three hundred sixty-six houses, and
on September 21 the newly elected county officials held
a meeting in Jacobsville, approved the shift of the
county seat to Austin, and moved there that afternoon—
taking the courthouse with them.

The overflow from Virginia City rapidly spilled into
Austin. On one day alone, nineteen passenger wagons,
three pack trains, and two hundred seventy-four freight
teams brought newcomers to Austin; sixty-nine men
showed up on horseback that day and thirty-one on
foot, besides. As mines sprouted along Pony Canyon
and stamp mills went into operation, this town halfway
to nowhere doubled and tripled in population from
week to week. Austin's International Hotel, which is
still standing, was constructed in part from material
taken from the hotel of the same name in Virginia City.
When Virginia City's original International Hotel gave
way to its imposing successor, its bar and structural
timbers were transported across the desert to Austin.
Samuel Bowles, the New England newspaperman who
toured Nevada in 1865, reached Austin at a time when

its first frantic growth was over, for he wrote in a book published in 1869 that Austin, which he called "the most representative mining town we had yet seen," had had a population of six to eight thousand in 1863, which "fell away in 1865 to four thousand, and now probably [is] no more than three thousand. Its houses are built anywhere, everywhere, and then the streets get to them as best they can; one side of a house will be four stories, the other one or two—such is the lay of the land; not a tree, not a flower, not a blade of green grass anywhere in town; but the boot-blacks and baths and barbers are of European standards; it has a first-class French restaurant and a daily newspaper; the handsomest woman, physically, I ever saw presided, with almost comic queenliness, over one of its lager beer saloons; gambling went on openly, amid music, in the area of every 'saloon' —miners risking to this chance at night the proceeds of the scarcely less doubtful chance of the day; while the generally cultivated and classical tone of the town may be inferred from this advertisement in the daily paper:

" 'Mammoth Lager Beer Saloon, in the basement, corner Main and Virginia streets, Austin, Nevada. Choice liquors, wines, lager beer and cigars, served by pretty girls, who understand their business and attend to it . . . .' "

In 1864 Austin was the scene of the famed "Sanitary Flour-Sack" affair, which Mark Twain describes in *Roughing It*. Reuel Gridley, a Missourian schoolmate of his who now was running a grocery store in Austin, ran for mayor on the Democratic ticket against Dr. H. S. Herrick, a Republican. Twain told how

> He and the Republican candidate made an agreement that the defeated man should be publicly presented with a fifty-pound sack of flour by the successful one, and should carry it home on his shoulder. Gridley was defeated. The new mayor gave him the sack of flour, and he shouldered it and carried it a mile or two, from Lower Austin to his home in Upper Austin, attended by a band of music and the whole population.

When he got there, Gridley remarked that he did not really need the flour, and asked the crowd what he should do with it. Someone called out that he should auction it off for the benefit of the United States Sanitary Commission, which was the Civil War equivalent of the Red Cross. At once Gridley mounted a box and began the auction.

> The bids went higher and higher, as the sympathies of the pioneers awoke and expanded, till at last the sack was knocked down to a mill-man at two hundred and fifty dollars, and his check taken. He was asked where he would have the flour delivered, and he said:
> "Nowhere—sell it again."
> Now the cheers went up royally, and the multitude were fairly in the spirit of the thing. So Gridley stood there and shouted and perspired till the sun went down; and when the crowd dispersed he had sold the sack to three hundred different people, and had taken in eight

thousand dollars in gold. And still the flour-sack was in his possession.

Twain tells how Virginia City heard the story and invited Gridley to conduct an auction there. He crossed the desert a couple of days later, but his efforts raised only $5,000. The leading citizens of Virginia City, embarrassed at being outdone by an upstart boom town like Austin, asked Gridley to remain and conduct a second auction the next day—and this time things were better organized:

> A procession of open carriages, attended by clamorous bands of music and adorned with a moving display of flags, filed along C Street and was soon in danger of blockade by a huzzaing multitude of citizens. In the first carriage sat Gridley, with the flour-sack in prominent view, the latter splendid with bright paint and gilt lettering; also in the same carriage sat the mayor and the recorder. The other carriages contained the Common Council, the editors and reporters, and other people of imposing consequence.

The cavalcade moved right out of Virginia City, to the surprise of the crowd, and on into neighboring Gold Hill, which had been warned in advance.

> We descended into Gold Hill with drums beating and colors flying, and enveloped in imposing clouds of dust. The whole population—men, women, and children, Chinamen, and Indians—were massed in the main street, all the flags in town were at the masthead, and the blare of the band was drowned in cheers. Gridley stood up

and asked who would make the first bid for the National Sanitary Flour-Sack. General W. said:

"The Yellow Jacket silver-mining company offers a thousand dollars, coin!"

Other bids followed, and within an hour Gridley had extracted a noble price from the small population of Gold Hill. Then he moved along, still keeping the sack, to the mining camps of Silver City and Dayton, where more money was raised. At half past eight in the evening the procession returned to Virginia City, which staged a torchlight parade as the prelude to the auction. At the end of two and a half hours, the flour sack had been sold for a total of $40,000 more—about $3 per inhabitant. "The grand total would have been twice as large," said Mark Twain, "but the streets were very narrow, and hundreds who wanted to bid could not get within a block of the stand, and could not make themselves heard."

Later the indefatigable Gridley auctioned the sack in Carson City, and then in California. After doing San Francisco he went on tour in the East, some said all the way to New York. "I am not sure of that," Twain's account concludes, "but I know that he finally carried it to St. Louis, where a monster sanitary fair was being held, and after selling it there for a large sum and helping on the enthusiasm by displaying the portly silver bricks which Nevada's donation had produced, he had the flour baked up into small cakes and retailed them at high prices." Altogether he spent three months selling the sack, covering more than fifteen thousand miles. "It was estimated that when the flour-sack's mission was ended it had been sold for a grand total of a hundred and fifty thousand dollars in greenbacks! This is probably the only instance on record where common family flour brought three thousand dollars a pound in the public market."

The going price for silver ore at Austin was somewhat lower, but the town did well all through the 1860's and early 1870's, enjoying some of its best years while Virginia City was producing little silver. But Austin's isolated position caused problems; it was costly to transport ore to the financial centers, and as the high-grade deposits were mined out it started to become uneconomical to work there. Only the coming of the railroad could save the town. The nearest rail line passed one hundred miles to the north; but in 1875 Austin succeeded in getting a county subsidy to build a connecting spur to the closest depot of that line, at Battle Mountain.

County authorities gave Austin five years to get its rail line built. If nothing were done in that time, the grant would expire and the $200,000 subsidy would be canceled. Over the next four and a half years, the citizens of Austin tried without luck to find someone interested in constructing the line. Finally, on August 30, 1879, an eastern mining syndicate agreed to do the work. Just five months were left before the county grant expired. Ground was broken at Battle Mountain on September 1, and as winter closed in the workmen struggled to reach Austin in time. The deadline neared. The railroad was still two miles from Austin at noon on February 9, 1880, with only twelve hours to go. Heavy snows hindered work; the train bringing the rails was stalled up the line. A day of frantic work saw rails being laid over snow and coming within half a mile of Austin's boundaries. The county grant specified that the road must actually reach Austin; so the city council held an emergency meeting that extended the city limits just far enough to reach the track. At ten minutes to midnight the track crossed the new boundary and all was well.

The railroad brought new vitality to Austin. Now that ore could be shipped cheaply, dozens of old mines were reopened and new ones were developed. As usual, boom was followed by bust; when the ground had given up its ore, Austin lost its reason for existing, and began gently to slide into ghostliness. The famous railroad to Battle Mountain, built with so much enthusiasm, went out of business after twenty-seven years; during its final few years it had carried no ore at all, and had averaged four passengers a month.

Austin's population today is minute. Travelers rush through it on Highway 50 without bothering to stop, for all they see is a dreary-looking old town. But the International Hotel is still there, and so is Gridley's store. The courthouse that was hauled up canyon from Jacobsville no longer exists, but the brick building that replaced it is itself of historic importance, for it was erected in 1869, during Austin's giddiest moments. A pamphlet put out by the people of Austin declares, "Its population has shrunken to a fraction of what it once was, and many of its buildings have deteriorated and fallen down, but in most respects Austin is much the same today as it was in the 'sixties. It has not been 'modernized' and its famous old Main Street is not lined with garish honkytonks. It is, in itself, an unspoiled relic of Nevada and the West in the days of their greatest fame and glory." But the cars zoom by, heading for the neon-lit thrills of the Lake Tahoe resort area and pay no heed.

In 1868 Austin gave rise to a daughter town one hundred twenty miles away whose career was as brilliant and as brief as a rocket's: the town of White Pine, which has vanished from the maps. Prospectors from Austin discovered the mines there, and the town was settled by emigrants from Austin; and when the excitement was over, most of White Pine's population moved back to Austin.

Fred Hart, one of the many gifted newspapermen of the old West, told the story of White Pine in a book called *The Sazerac Lying Club*, published in San Francisco in 1878. This was mostly a collection of tall tales, but he also included some straightforward journalistic pieces, including his account of the Fourth of July celebration at White Pine. Hart was a roving prospector and part-time man of letters who worked for a while in Montana in the 1860's, then moved on to Nevada, enjoyed a brief stint as editor of the Virginia City *Enterprise*, and finished his career in California. He was living in Austin in 1868 when the first ore samples from White Pine came in, and wrote that

> It was not necessary that a person should be an expert to determine that the rock was rich. A man who had never in his life seen a silver mine, or never before handled a piece of silver ore, could tell at a glance that it was metal. It came pretty near being pure silver, some of the "horn-silver" specimens being so heavy and metallic that they could be converted into bullion by the simple process of melting in a crucible. Ever on the alert for a new camp, I had no sooner seen these specimens than I determined to go to White Pine.

He made the trip on horseback in two and a half days. The mines were located in a 9,000-foot-high mountain called Treasure Hill, and two camps were in existence nearby: the town of Hamilton, at the foot of the western and southern slopes of the mountain, and the town of Treasure City, on the mountain itself. "At the time of my arrival," Hart wrote, "there was considerable rivalry as to which of the two camps should be the future metropolis of White Pine. The mines were marvelously rich, and the prospects were that they were extensive; and it was evident that the district was destined to receive a large population ere long—so, of course, it must have a city." The hill people urged the settlement to be placed up there, for they were "squatted right down on the top of the mines." But the citizens of Hamilton scoffed at that idea, since there was no water supply on the mountain, and not nearly as much room for a large city there as on the level plateau at its foot. Besides, they argued, Hamilton already had a head start: Treasure City consisted of nothing more than a few tents, while Hamilton had three or four stone cabins, some seventy-five inhabitants, and a large tent in which some men from Austin had started "an establishment combining store, saloon, restaurant, lodging-house, post-office, and express office." In the end both sides held firm where they were, and White Pine was founded as a double city, comprising the towns of Hamilton and Treasure City.

The rivalry was intense—so much so that the people of one town had as little as possible to do with those of the other. But July 4, 1868, was approaching, and patriotism demanded a proper celebration. Hart tells us,

The inhabitants of each town held a public meeting, at which committees of arrangements and officers of the day were appointed, and resolutions adopted that each town would hold a celebration on its own hook, independent and entirely oblivious of even the existence of

145

the other. Better counsels prevailed, however, when on "counting noses" it was found that there was not a sufficient number of men in each camp for two celebrations, and that the only way in which an air of respectability could be secured for the occasion was by fusing the forces and holding a joint celebration. A compromise was effected, by the terms of which Treasure City was to have the poet of the day and the chairman to preside over the literary exercises. Hamilton was to have the other offices, and the meeting and the "ball in the evening" were to be held in that town; but it was stipulated that the citizens of Hamilton were to march in procession up to Treasure City, meet the citizens of that metropolis drawn up in line to await their coming, and escort them in procession back to Hamilton.

Hart, who was living in Hamilton, was named a member of the Committee on Flag, Music, and Ball in the Evening. The committee had some difficult problems. The nearest American flag was in Austin, and no one could make the two hundred and forty-mile round trip in the forty-eight hours allowed for preparations. It was easy enough to arrange for the music and the ball in the evening, for Hamilton had a man called Pike who could play one tune, "the Arkansaw Traveler," on the fiddle; Pike could also call square dances. But what would the Fourth of July be without an American flag? The female population of White Pine—numbering two, both residents of Hamilton—agreed to manufacture a flag if Hart would provide material of the right color.

There was plenty of white cloth in the store, used for making tents. That would take care of the stars and the white stripes. The red stripes could be produced by cutting up red flannel shirts. But there had to be a blue background for the stars, and there was no blue cloth anywhere in the two towns. In the course of his investigations, Hart came upon an "aristocrat" who had a quilt on his bed, lined with red calico. This he confiscated at once, making it unnecessary to cut up shirts, but no blue fabric whatever appeared. He relates that "the committee sat in solemn council, debating the propriety of making the field of the flag out of a gray shirt, and taking the chances that the vivid imagination of the beholder might give it a blue hue, as the emblem of our liberties floated from the ninety-foot pole which the Committee on Pole had already erected . . . ."

While the possibilities of a red, white, and gray Stars and Stripes were being debated, "a courier arrived at the council and announced that a family of Mormons had just arrived and were making camp in a little ravine below our embryo city—and there were four girls and an old woman in the outfit, too." It was exciting news. The five Mormon females must surely have one blue dress among them; and the sudden multiplication of the local female population would do much to balance the proportions of the sexes at the square dance. Hart immediately went down to the Mormons to inform them of White Pine's problems. He found the head of the party and a couple of boys building a shack out of poles and blankets, while the mother and girls were preparing supper at a campfire.

Hart tipped his hat, bowed, and said, "Good evening, Madam."

"The old lady," he reported, "was very large, fat, and ungainly. She was so busy with her cooking that she had not noticed my presence in the camp till I addressed her as above stated." In surprise she swung around, toppled, and hurled her frying-pan in the air, "shedding a shower of slices of sizzling bacon, one of which struck the oldest girl on the back of her neck, and slid down inside her dress. The girl set up a yell that would have done credit to Sitting Bull . . . ." The Mormon father, ax upraised, rushed over to find out what Hart was doing to his women. Shakily Hart explained his mission; the Mormon women grew calmer, rummaged in their trunks, and produced an old blue veil. It was, the mother said, of great sentimental value, but she told Hart that he could have it for $5. That seemed a fair price, she remarked, in a place "where the mines were so rich that the silver was sticking right up out of the top of the ground."

Hart paid the price and took the veil up to Hamilton. The members of the committee put the finishing touches on the flag, and Hart went back to the Mormons to invite them to the ceremonies and the square dance. Unhappily, the girls owned no shoes, and the ballroom floor was unplaned and full of splinters; but Hamilton's store yielded "a sufficient number of men's cowhide brogans to shoe the Mormon girls, and thus was another difficulty overcome."

On the morning of the Fourth of July the improvised flag was hoisted with appropriate shouts and cheers, and the men of Hamilton lined up, two by two, to march to Treasure City. In the absence of a brass band, "two of the best whistlers in camp walked in front and whistled 'Yankee Doodle' till the steep ascent and light atmosphere took away their breath. Arrived on the hill, they were met by the citizens of Treasure City, who, after the formalities of the reception were gone through in the nearest saloon, also fell in line, and the combined forces of the two towns marched in procession back to Hamilton."

There the day's literary exercises commenced: an oration by the orator of the day, a poem by the poet of the day, and the singing of patriotic songs "by the congregation." Afterward a Society of White Pine Pioneers was organized, and a resolution adopted that the flag then flying from the pole outside "should form a part of the Society's archives, that future generations might know the difficulties, hardships, and privations with which the pioneers of White Pine District and the founders of the city of Hamilton had been beset in their endeavors to properly celebrate the anniversary of the nation's independence."

The grand ball that evening was held in an unfinished building, forty feet by twenty, intended for eventual use as a store. Since it lacked a roof and two of its walls at the moment, a cloth canopy was draped over the tops of the two existing walls. Against one of the cloth façades thus created sat the fiddler Pike on a three-legged stool, playing his one tune while the square-dancers galloped about. The Mormon girls danced well, and Pike played for all he was worth, pausing occasionally to refresh himself in the saloon tent next door. Hart wrote:

> Everybody seemed to enjoy the occasion, till an unforeseen and calamitous incident cast a pall of gloom over the festivities, and broke up the affair . . . . The dancers were in the midst of a quadrille, when suddenly the music grew faint in sound, and the "calls" ceased. The fiddler had suddenly and mysteriously disappeared. Wonder and curiosity were depicted on every face in the ball-room, but the overturned stool, which had been the orchestra stand, and notes of the "Arkansaw Traveler" welling up faintly from the rear of the building, told the awful tale. Pike, in an effort to put some artistic variations, had leaned back against the treacherous cloth wall, lost his equilibrium, and dropped out of sight through the wall to the ground below. A number of men rushed out to the rear of the house to recover the orchestra, but when they got to him he was just passing into a peaceful sleep, his right hand spasmodically working the fiddle-bow, which lay across his left shoulder, and the expiring notes of the "Arkansaw Traveler" dying

on the air. All efforts to arouse him were fruitless, and as he was the only man in the camp who could fiddle, the "ball in the evening" was at its end.

Shortly after the epic Fourth of July celebration, White Pine's big boom got under way. By September of 1868, a twenty-five by one hundred lot in town sold for as much as $25,000; buildings went up overnight, streets were laid out, banks and express offices opened, stores offered every sort of merchandise. One of the casualties of this wild growth was the historic flag that had been assembled with such great effort. The archives of the Society of White Pine Pioneers had been deposited with a local storekeeper, who during the boom opened a lodging house in his shop. Hart noted that

> This department consisted of tiers of bunks ranged along the rear of the store, each bunk being furnished with a coarse, straw-filled tick, two pair of blankets, and a rude pillow. These bunks were rented out to weary travelers and hopeful pilgrims to the new mines at the reasonable rental of two dollars per night, with the privilege of a free cocktail at the bar on arising in the morning. One night an aristocratic capitalist from San Francisco put up at the lodging-house, and had the effrontery to demand a pair of sheets on his bed. The proprietor of the establishment was almost struck dumb with amaze at this outrageous request; but then, the man was a capitalist, and was from San Francisco, and it might be against the interest of the mining resources of the district for him to become offended . . . . The landlord

had no sheets, and there were, in all probability, none to be had in the camp, but he was equal to the emergency. He went to the archives of the Society of White Pine Pioneers, and took therefore its only archive—to wit, the flag—and tore it in half and spread the two pieces on the bed to be occupied by the high-toned capitalist.

Thereafter, that bunk was reserved for the exclusive use of visitors from San Francisco, who were charged fifty cents extra for occupying it. In time the flag was in sorry disrepair, and Hart says, "the last that I saw of the starry emblem . . . a couple of Shoshone squaws were each wearing a piece of it over their shoulders for a shawl."

Scores of more elegant flags waved from the flagstaffs of White Pine as it celebrated the Fourth of July under vastly altered circumstances in 1869. Hart said:

Where the handful of coarsely-clothed prospectors had marched in procession the year before, now marched a grand pageant—military companies; a fire department, with handsome, costly, and beautiful decorated engines and hose carriages; a car of state, containing bright-faced and gaily-attired girls, representing the various States in the Union; brass bands, streamers, brightness, and beauty . . . . The line of the procession of the year before, over a mere trail through the brush, with only a few poor tents and cabins marking the site of the town, was now a broad street, with handsome two- and three-story structures of brick and stone, built compactly on each side.

A thousand onlookers cheered the marchers on; and that night "hundreds of richly dressed and jeweled women" lent glamor and glitter to the excitement of the Independence Day ball.

It was a magnificent moment—the greatest day in White Pine's brief history, for, Hart relates,

> White Pine went down almost as rapidly as it came up. The mines petered and the bubble bursted. Today, Hamilton and Treasure City are both insignificant and nearly depopulated camps; the few who remain in them have clung on, hoping on, hoping ever, for a strike in the mines that shall bring a return of something like the good old times of the early days.

Equally brilliant and nearly as brief was the career of Aurora, Nevada, a spectacular mining town of the 1860's that time has reduced to nothing more than a heap of rubble. Three prospectors working east of California's Mono Lake were hunting for game late in August 1860, when one man picked up a chunk of interesting-looking quartz. With the giddy example of newly founded Virginia City before their eyes, they staked out seven claims and hurried to Monoville to file the required official notice with the town recorder. A few days later, they went back to their claims—accompanied now by a horde of comrades—and founded the Esmeralda mining district, ten miles square.

Before long the assayer in Carson City handed down

his verdict on their ore samples: an unusually high concentration of silver was present, rivaling the richest ore of the Comstock Lode. At once, nearly the whole population of Monoville took up lodgings on Esmeralda Hill. This turned out to be unsatisfactory as a town site, and the men moved to lower ground and laid out a camp they called Aurora. The arrival of winter put a stop to any mining activities, but by the spring of 1861 the town was swarming with prospectors.

A curious political problem arose. Was Aurora in California or was it in Nevada? The boundary between California and Nevada in those parts was then only vaguely defined, pending a careful survey. In March 1861, California set up Mono County, with Aurora as the county seat. Seven months later the Nevada Territorial Legislature created Esmeralda County—naming Aurora as the county seat. All through 1862 and most of 1863 overlapping county governments were avoided through a friendly agreement that the area would be considered part of California until the boundary surveyors had done their work.

The time for the 1863 county elections approached with the surveyors still some distance away. So a double set of elections was held, one under Nevada jurisdiction and one under that of California. The Aurora voters cast their ballots at the police station for Mono County officials, and at the local armory for the officials of Esmeralda County. On September 22 the surveyors placed the boundary four miles west of Aurora, making it formally part of Nevada. Aurora's set of Nevada officials took charge, and the California officials packed up their records and headed for the nearest California town, Bodie, twelve miles to the west.

The mines of Aurora yielded a bonanza of silver during those years. Six major mines kept seventeen stamp mills busy crushing the rich ore, and by 1864 the popu-

lation reached ten thousand. Solid brick buildings went up on the main streets; and it was a measure of Aurora's wealth that all the brick was imported from the East, shipped around Cape Horn and hauled inland from California. Silver production reach several million dollars a year during the Civil War era.

The war itself was far away from the western mining camps, where slavery was not a serious issue and eastern events seemed unreal and remote. Yet there were fierce debates in Aurora between the loyal Union men—who formed a large majority—and the few miners who came from the Confederate states. Feelings grew so high that the southerners were forced at gunpoint to swear allegiance to the Union flag. As in Austin and Virginia City, auctions were held for the benefit of the sanitary commission. Gridley and his flour sack never got to Aurora, but the Wide West Mining Company donated a fifty-pound sample of ore containing several hundred dollars' worth of gold and silver. Major E. A. Sherman, the owner of the local newspaper, auctioned the ore off many times. Eventually he took it East with him and traded it to the town of Plymouth, Massachusetts, for a small piece of the Plymouth Rock. This relic of pioneer days in New England was cemented into the wall of Aurora's courthouse.

Aurora, like most of the mining camps, had its full share of bandits, murderers, and other desperadoes. When matters got particularly rough in the spring of

1864, the better class of citizens appointed a vigilance committee, collected the criminals, and sentenced four of the worst offenders to death. News of this improvised legal system reached Territorial Governor Nye, who upon learning that a hanging was to take place in Aurora sent a telegram urgently insisting that no acts of violence be committed. Back came the reply: "All quiet and orderly. Four men will be hung in half an hour." After that, Aurora's crime problems were greatly diminished.

So, alas, were Aurora's mines. By the end of 1864 the best of the ore was gone and, with $27,000,000 in bullion already shipped out, little remained to be unearthed. Lawsuits over conflicting claims tied up the few mines that were not exhausted. Population dropped, and Aurora ceased to be the county seat of Esmeralda County. By 1880 only five hundred citizens lingered on. The Esmeralda *Herald* managed some optimistic thoughts in its edition of September 15, 1883:

> There is no star that sets, but that will rise again to illuminate another sky. Aurora is taking on new life . . . . Her ancient pride seems to be returning in the way of renewed activity in her mines. Work has been resumed on the Great Republic. The Silver Hill mill is working . . . .
>
> There has never been a lack of ore in Aurora; it has always been held back for want of capital and since the people can't get the mountain to come to them they have resolved to do the next best, work and prove their great worth. A contract to sink a shaft 100 feet deep on the

Silver Lining, west of the Humbolt has been let. A few more pushers on the wheel and Aurora will resume her place of twenty years ago.

This revival proved to be overambitious. The re-opened mines produced very little, and two weeks later the *Herald* commented, "The few citizens of this place amuse themselves by going from store to store, saloon to saloon to tell each other how dull it is."

Thirty years of slumber followed. In 1914 the Aurora Consolidated Mines Company began to haul ore from some of the old mines, and for four years there was activity in the town; but in 1918 the company gave up, dismantled its stamp mill, and took its equipment off to another site many miles away. By 1930 the population of Aurora was one. In time that last lonely Auroran was gathered to his reward, and the 1950 census failed to show any residents whatever. Even the sturdy brick buildings, which had withstood the onslaught of the elements so bravely for nearly a century, were demolished; they were torn down so that their fine bricks could be taken off to Reno and sold by salvagers at $65 a thousand. Only stumps and fragments remain of Aurora today: part of the courthouse, a section of the Wells Fargo building, a schoolhouse, and two weed-choked cemeteries. The triumph of time is nearly complete.

SEVEN
On to the Rockies

Almost at the same time that Nevada's great silver rush was getting under way, the Colorado Rockies beckoned to those who sought gold. The Colorado boom was born out of fantasy and fancy headlines, for the pioneer explorers of what was then the western part of Kansas Territory had not really discovered much gold. William Green Russell, an unsuccessful forty-niner from Georgia, started the Colorado boom in the summer of 1858 when he and a few friends went prospecting near Pike's Peak, Colorado. Somewhat to the north of the big mountain they found small amounts of placer gold. It was not a spectacular find, and they moved on down the eastern slopes of the Rockies and kept going all the way to what is now Wyoming, without much success anywhere.

Yet distorted and magnified accounts of their explorations found their way eastward. Newspapers announced,

A NEW ELDORADO IN KANSAS TERRITORY.

Times were hard back East, where business was still in the grip of the panic of 1857, and thousands of greenhorns began to entertain dreams of Colorado's riches. In the winter of 1858-59 they gathered in large groups at such eastern assembly points as Kansas City, Omaha, and Independence, inspired by the wildly exaggerated stories emanating from Colorado. And when spring came they set out. "Pike's Peak or Bust" was their slogan.

Meanwhile Russell and his friends had decided early in 1859 that there was more future in Colorado real estate than in Colorado gold, and had laid out the town of Denver, planning to make their fortunes selling lots to the hordes of hopeful "fifty-niners." When the newcomers arrived, the promoters were ready for them. About 100,000 had set out for Colorado. Half of these turned back, "busted," before they reached the supposed land of gold. Of the others, some 25,000 settled in Colorado and the rest stayed just long enough to learn that the gold of Colorado was largely a myth. They headed angrily for home, muttering about fraud and humbug, and thus they missed out on the real Colorado gold strikes.

While thousands of would-be miners were pouring into Denver in the spring of '59, a few experienced prospectors were making rich discoveries on a pair of creeks some miles west of the new city. George A. Jackson, a veteran forty-niner, found a respectable gold mine on Chicago Creek in January, but kept quiet about it until April. John H. Gregory, another old-time prospector, struck it rich on nearby Clear Creek on May 6. He scooped up a pan of dirt, found $4 worth of gold in it, and followed the "color" up a gulch until he came upon a vein of gold running through quartz. In a few days he collected gold worth nearly a thousand dollars, and then headed for Denver to file his claim and spread the news. Shortly he agreed to sell his claim for $21,000, and vanished from history.

Prospectors streamed toward Gregory Gulch. The discovery of gold there turned the Colorado boom from a fiasco into a California-style bonanza. The new gold rush was helped notably by publicity from several eastern journalists who, by coincidence, visited Gregory Gulch a month after the discovery. The most famous of these was Horace Greeley, the mild-mannered, bewhiskered editor of the New York *Tribune,* who had been touring California and Nevada in 1859 and was on his way back to civilization when he heard of the Colorado gold strike. Alice Polk Hill's *Tales of the Colorado Pioneers*, published in Denver in 1884, tells of Greeley's adventures in the land of gold:

> When he arrived in Denver he was received with all the honor that the infant city could command. He said

he didn't intend to be deceived in this matter, that seeing was believing, and he wanted to wash out some of the dirt himself. So the men put their heads together to see how they could "come it" over the old gentleman. They themselves were satisfied as to the richness of Gregory Gulch, it was no intention to deceive, but Solomon says "there is a time for all things," and they wanted a "good one" on Horace Greeley. So they sent a message to the camp that Horace was coming, and to salt a mine.

The boys took down an old shotgun and fired gold dust into a hole for all it was worth.

Bright and early the next morning a spanking team was rigged up, and the distinguished gentleman started for the gulch, accompanied by some of the most plausible, entertaining and versatile talkers of the country. They escorted him over the diggings, related all the interesting events in the history of its discovery, showed him specimens of the dirt and the pure gold that had been washed out. Mr. Greeley's soul was in arms, and, eager for the task, he called for a shovel and pan, rolled up his sleeves, and went down into the pit. They gave him all the necessary instructions as to the process of panning, and looked on with palpitating anxiety.

Mr. Greeley was an apt scholar, and put his dirt through like an adept in the art. It panned out big. All the bottom of the pan was covered with bright gold particles. They slapped him on the shoulders in regular Western style, and told him to try it again—which he did, with the same success. Then he gathered up his gold dust in a bag and said:

"Gentlemen, I have worked with my own hands and seen with my own eyes, and the news of your rich dis-

covery shall go all over the world, as far as my paper can waft it."

Mr. Greeley left, believing he had made a thorough test. As soon as he reached New York he devoted a whole side of the *Tribune* to an ecstatic description of the camp, headed with large, glaring type, such as 'bill-stickers' use. The report was read all over the country, and caused a great rush to the land of promise. Those who had the fever took a relapse, and they had it bad. It was a raging epidemic, and spread faster than the cholera in Egypt.

He shouted into the ears of the over-crowded East until the welkin rang, "Young man, go West!" It was his glowing articles and earnest advice about "going West" that caused the first great boom in Colorado. The honest old man went down to his grave ignorant of the joke that was played upon him.

By September of 1859, the tents and cabins of 900 prospectors had risen along the sides of Gregory Gulch. The weekly take of gold was averaging about $50,000. The first settlement was called Gregory Point, which changed its name after a few months to Mountain City. A second town, called Black Hawk, was founded about a mile below Mountain City. But miners tended to collect high in the gulch itself, even though this was not an ideal place for a town, and in the summer of 1860 the collection of shanties and tents near the mines adopted the name of Central City. Central City quickly became the metropolis of the region. Far above the city streets mine shafts were driven into the slopes and a golden yield emerged from what soon was being called "the richest square mile on earth." Within a few years Central City was second only to Denver in size among Colorado's cities. That was not saying a great deal, since the population of Denver as late as 1870 was all of 4,759. But considering that Colorado had been inhabited only by a few Indians until 1858, the growth had been rapid.

Central City attracted the colorful, raffish mining-camp types; Denver, which was not a mining camp but a business center, tended to draw bankers, merchants, and stockbrokers. One of Central City's leading figures was Pat Casey, who was originally a hired hand working in the Ben Burroughs mine, discovered in 1859. Casey bought a little property of his own, and in 1862 an accidental cave-in exposed a vein of rich ore there and made him a wealthy man overnight. He invested $1,500 in a pair of handsome black horses and drove them along the steep streets of Central City; when a tax assessor asked him their value, he proudly declared them at $2,500 and refused to pay tax on them at any lower rate. Visiting New York once, he feared getting lost in a big hotel's corridors, and blazed a trail for himself from hall to hall —drawing a bill for $2,000 for repairs. The street leading from downtown Central City to the Ben Burroughs mine was named "The Casey" in his honor. One night in a cheerful mood he walked down The Casey to the shaft of his mine, pulled a bottle of whiskey from his pocket, peered over the edge, and yelled to his workmen, "How many of yez are down there?"

"Five," came a distant voice.

Casey thought this over for a moment and called back, "Well, half of yez come up and have a drink."

The mines of Central City had the common habit of filling up with water from underground seepage if they were left unworked for a while. A specialist in unwatering the local mine shafts was Gassy Thompson, who sometimes found that he had taken on a harder pumping job than he cared to do. One such time he stood for a long while contemplating a mine that was flooded with several hundred feet of water until a bright idea occurred. A stray dog happened by, and Gassy felled it with a stone. He found an old hat and coat lying near the mouth of the mine and smeared some of the dog's blood on it. Then he tied a rock around the dog, dropped it into the mine, and waited until he heard the splash from the depths. His next step was to go down to Central City and spread a rumor through the saloons of foul play at that mine. Soon word was getting around that bloodstained clothing had been found up there. The sheriff organized a posse and went to investigate. There certainly was room for suspicion, so the posse borrowed some pumps and set to work pumping the shaft dry to find the body. The body was there, all right—the body of the dog.

Gassy Thompson had shrewdly taken off for another county. He stayed out of sight until the anger of the sheriff and his men had cooled. Then he showed up to collect his fee from the owners of the shaft. He had fulfilled his contract, after all; the mine had been unwatered.

The first newspaper in Gregory Gulch was *The Rocky Mountain Gold Reporter*, which had a six-week run in 1859. Three years later Central City's *Miners' Register* was founded. Its owner, Alfred Thompson, brought a press and type in from Iowa and built a two-story newspaper office late in 1862. The paper is still being published on the second floor of that building, although now it is known as the *Register-Call,* and a third floor has been added to the building. In the early days, the *Register* was occasionally printed on wrapping paper when supplies of newsprint heading West on wagons were burned by Indians. (Once the paper came out printed on wallpaper.) The early editions tell of cultural events in the mining town and of Central City's isolation from the East:

> Artemus Ward, world renowned humorist and comic lecturer, arrived in Denver and on Thursday night will be with his mountain friends to "speak his piece" . . . and enlighten us on the mysteries of the show business . . . . (*Register*, February 24, 1864.)
>
> An eastern mail is expected constantly. It is so long since we had eastern mail that we had forgotten almost that our correspondence lived. (September 15, 1864.)
>
> The Missouri River has been so full of ice for several days past that the mails could not be got over. (December 4, 1864.)
>
> The Down Coach was upset yesterday by running off the bridge at the Dickerson mill. It fell upon the top causing the passengers to fall on their heads. There were nine passengers inside. H. M. Teller was severely bruised and cut . . . . The driver . . . laid senseless for some time. He is now at the Pacific House and is recovering. The accident occurred because of the very slippery condition of the road. (December 8, 1864.)

On April 15, 1865, news of the assassination of President Lincoln reached Central City by telegraph. The *Register* at once prepared to put out a black-bordered memorial issue, for Central City and her men had been overwhelmingly loyal to the Union in the Civil War. But a certain William Taber, newly arrived from Kentucky, had Confederate sympathies. He was heard to declare, "I'm glad of it. Served him right." Shocked citizens gathered and yelled that this insult to Lincoln's memory should be avenged by a prompt lynching. Sheriff Bill Cozzens arrested Taber to protect him from the fury of the mob. The city authorities sent a telegram to the military administration in Denver, asking for advice. Brigadier General Patrick E. Connor replied, "Turn him over to the people to do with him as they please. If they do not want to deal with him send him here in irons."

By late afternoon it looked as though the townspeople were getting ready to break into the jail and string Taber up. Sheriff Cozzens conferred with the town's leading lawyer, Henry M. Teller—the same man who had been bruised and cut in the December stagecoach accident. Teller and the sheriff called a meeting at which the lawyer told the mob that a lynching would be a "lasting disgrace on the town" and urged them "to abandon their bloody purpose." Tempers subsided and Taber was given a formal trial. The *Register* reported on April 27 that "Taber, the southern sympathizer, has been condemned at Denver and sentenced to carry a bag of sand weighing sixty pounds, six hours a day for thirty days."

Central City's first theater was a log cabin down the gulch in the suburb of Mountain City, which used candles for footlights. In 1860 it was joined by the People's Theater, whose proprietor, Charley Switz, described it as the "first well ordered and respectable place for theatrical entertainment in the city." Two years later George Harrison opened the National Theater on Main Street. He did not get along well with Charley Switz, and finally shot his competitor from the front balcony of the National. Harrison was tried for murder, acquitted, and staged a successful season of drama before going South to join the Confederate army. The theater was sold and its name was changed to the Montana.

In 1865 *Uncle Tom's Cabin* was presented there, using elaborate scenery brought from the East. The *Register*'s review on July 21 declared that among the roles "everybody has noticed that of Eva as personified by Master Benny Wheeler . . . with face upturned to heaven and eyes filling with tears, his appeals to his parents for the freedom of Uncle Tom is sublimely beautiful."

On June 24, 1872, an elegant four-story hotel opened on Eureka Street and immediately became the center of the town's social life. It was named the Teller House, in honor of Central City's most distinguished citizen. According to the *Register*, invitations to an opening-night celebration were sent "to nearly a hundred citizens of Central and vicinity. Most of them came, many with their ladies. After dinner the party assembled in the spacious parlors where a few brief speeches were made, garnished with exquisite music by Professor Barnum's orchestra.

"Across the main hall and opposite the office is the billiard rooms and bar . . . well supplied with things to cheer and inebriate.

"All sleeping rooms to the number of ninety are tastefully fitted with all essential conveniences. The majority are . . . without transoms, ventilation being obtained by adjustable windows. Guests may therefore lie down to peaceful slumbers undisturbed by apprehensions of getting their heads blown off or valuables lifted by burglars."

The Teller House received a noteworthy guest in the spring of 1873: Ulysses S. Grant, the President of the United States. Some grand gesture seemed appropriate for the occasion. Paving the streets with gold was suggested, but gold was too commonplace a substance in Central City, so the town fathers borrowed $12,000 worth of silver bricks from a mine twenty miles away and laid them from the hotel door to the street. The President, says the *Register,* "was quite incredulous when told that the slabs were genuine silver; but had finally to accept the truth."

Central City was ravaged by fire in 1874. The blaze

began in the jumbled shacks of the Chinese district and swept through the city, leaving only six of the important buildings standing. The Register Block, as the newspaper office was called, was saved by cutting away its wooden cornice and dousing the roof constantly with water. The Teller House employees hung wet blankets on its windows and kept the grand hotel from going up, although the sashes and frames of the windows were charred and every pane was melted or broken. A town in the valley sent its fire company and equipment to Central City by train. Unfortunately the railroad reached only as far as the town of Black Hawk, two miles away, and the fire-fighters could not get to Central City in time to do much good.

After the fire many handsome new buildings were constructed, including the Belvidere Theater, where plays and operas were performed. The Belvidere did not seem quite adequate for large productions, though, and the citizens discussed putting up a glamorous opera house. Public contributions provided funds for the opera house, with the biggest donations coming from the Teller family. (When Colorado achieved statehood in 1876, it elected Henry M. Teller to the United States Senate.) On March 4, 1878, the Teller Opera House had its grand opening, and during the next twenty years every important actor and singer who toured the West made an appearance in its excellently designed auditorium.

Central City's fortunes rose and fell with the varying output of Gregory Gulch. By the middle of the 1860's, all the placer gold had been mined and the surface deposits were just about gone. The underlying quartz was too hard for the local stamp mills to crush, and a depression set in. Colorado produced almost $3,500,000 worth of gold per year in 1862 and 1863, most of it coming from the vicinity of Central City and the neighboring diggings along Clear Creek and Chicago Creek. But from 1864 to 1868 production was at a minimum.

The population of Colorado, which had grown from zero to 34,000 between 1858 and 1860, was no higher than 39,000 ten years later, and the dizzying early expansion of Central City and Denver halted almost entirely during those years. Samuel Bowles described the situation in his book of 1869, *Our New West:*

> When we first visited the country, in 1865, the original era of speculation, of waste, of careless and unintelligent work, and as little of it as possible, of living by wit instead of labor, of reliance upon eastern capital instead of home industry, was, if not at its height, still reigning, but with signs of decay and threatening despair. In the next two years, 1866 and 1867, affairs became desperate; the population shrunk; mines were abandoned; mills stopped; eastern capital, tired of waiting for promised returns, dried up its fountains; and the secrets of the rich ores seemed unfathomable.

Bowles goes on to tell how hard times forced the Colorado miners to adopt the Yankee virtues he prized so greatly. "Economy and work were enforced on all," and those who disliked frugal living went elsewhere.

> Thus weeded out, thus stimulated, the population fell back on the certainties; such mining as was obviously remunerative was continued; the doubtful and losing abandoned; the old and simple dirt washing for gold was resumed, and followed with more care; and farming rose in respectability and promise . . . . The main fact of the new era was that the people went to work, became self-reliant, and, believing they "had a good thing" out there,

undertook to prove it to the world by intelligent and economic industry.

Intelligence and industry were perhaps not as important to Central City's rebirth in the 1870's as the arrival of improved techniques for separating gold from rock. Carloads of gold once more came from the hills around Gregory Gulch: Silver Hill, Quartz Hill, Bobtail Hill, and on top the Glory Hole, 500 feet across and 900 feet deep, where gold was blasted out in great explosions. Colorado's gold output, which had dropped under a million dollars in 1867, doubled in 1868 and reached $3,000,000 in 1869. During the 1870's the mines at Central City alone yielded $2,000,000 a year in gold. Production continued well into the 1890's at almost the same rate, though at last the time came when it no longer paid to extract the ore.

By then Central City had been overshadowed by other Colorado boom camps. Silver, not gold, became the important metal. Colorado's output of silver exceeded that of gold after 1874, and a hearty silver rush began in 1877 with the discovery of spectacular mines at the misnamed town of Leadville. Within a year and a half Leadville grew from a tiny village to a city of fifteen thousand, with twenty-eight miles of streets and its own opera house to rival that of Central City. Leadville became the silver capital of the West for a while, stealing the show from Virginia City and her played-out Comstock Lode, and when the silver was gone there too, Leadville continued to flourish on the mining of copper, zinc, and lead. By 1890 it was gold in the headlines again, with a rich strike at Cripple Creek on the western slope of Pike's Peak. The price of silver fell sharply in 1893 as a result of government interference in the metals trade, wiping out most of the silver camps; but Cripple Creek kept Colorado wealthy with an endless outpouring of gold. By the year 1897 Colorado was producing more gold than California, and as the new century began it was responsible for one-third of the nation's total output of gold and silver. Colorado is still one of the most important mining states, though mining itself is far less significant to the country's economy now than it was in the nineteenth century.

Central City survived all shifts of fortune. Her population dropped from a peak of about seven thousand until by the turn of the century she was little more than a ghost town, but there were always some who remained faithful to her. While Denver, thirty miles to the east, became a mighty metropolis, Central City was able merely to hang on. The tightly packed rows of brick and stone houses, strung along the two main thoroughfares, remained. Almost all of the mine buildings and mills were torn down, and some of the business and residential streets, but even after the final shutdown of the mines in 1914 enough of the original town stayed alive to give visitors some idea of what Central City had been like in her heyday.

In 1932 a restoration program began. Today Central City has only a few hundred permanent inhabitants, but in the summer she becomes the destination of thousands of sightseers. Antique shops, art galleries, and restaurants try to maintain an "old West" flavor. The *Register* still is published from its century-old office. Opulent meals are served in the gilded second-floor dining room of the Teller House. A summer festival of plays and operas keeps the gaiety of the Teller Opera House alive. The Coeur d'Alene Mining Museum preserves the shaft of one of the original mines, the hoist that operated the ore buckets, the mine tracks and the ore cars that once traveled along them, the old steam engine and air compressor, and the blacksmith's forge where the drills were sharpened. The saloons and restaurants use chairs and furnishings dating from the 1870's. It is possible— almost—to stand on one of the twisting steep streets, close one's eyes, and hear the rumble of ore wagons, the shouts of the miners, the raucous tunes of the honkytonk pianists in the busy saloons. And for a moment it is as if no time had passed at all in Gregory Gulch since Horace Greeley was telling young men to go West.

EIGHT

The Prospectors Head North

NEW TRAILS ALWAYS AWAITED the seekers of buried treasure. The West seemed endless, and one never stopped hoping that the hills just beyond these would yield the sparkle of pay dirt. One by one the empty territories of the West had their mining crazes, gave birth to glamorous but short-lived towns, and went through the cycle of boom and bust.

California, Nevada, and Colorado all were settled originally by prospectors. Utah was different. The first Americans who came there were Mormons trying to escape religious persecution in the East, and they had very little interest in gold and silver.

The Mormons—more formally known as the Church of Jesus Christ of the Latter-day Saints—were followers of the young prophet Joseph Smith, who as a farm boy in New York State in the 1820's had seen visions of angels and had heard tales of otherwise unknown historic events. Guided by an angel, Joseph Smith said, he dug up golden plates in a hill near his home and translated the hieroglyphics with which they were inscribed. This translation was published as *The Book of Mormon* in 1830—an account, in biblical language, of the adventures of a party of Israelites that had escaped from Jerusalem in 600 B.C. and, so Joseph Smith asserted, had come to the New World.

The Book of Mormon became the scripture of a new religion. Joseph Smith converted first a few of his friends, then others in his neighborhood, until the so-called Mormons amounted to a considerable band. The beliefs and the customs of the Mormons were offensive to Christians of the older sects, and the persecution of the new creed was often violent. Joseph Smith himself was killed by an angry mob in 1844 while he was endeavoring to establish a colony for his people in Illinois. Brigham Young, his successor, realized that the Mormons would be safe only if they went far from their enemies, and the following year he led thousands of the Latter-day Saints on an exodus into the unknown West. This remarkable movement terminated in Utah, by the shores of Great Salt Lake. There, amid harsh surroundings not very different geographically from those encountered by the Hebrews when they entered Palestine, the Mormons founded a city and took possession of the otherwise uninhabited region. They dominate the life of Utah to this day.

Brigham Young feared that gold fever would lead his people into temptation. He did not want to see gold discovered in Utah, for that would surely bring a rush of Gentiles (as the Mormons called all those not of their faith) into the territory, renewing the old hostilities. And he felt that the Mormons would do better spending their energy in farming and ranching than in prospecting. "We cannot eat silver and gold," he said, "neither do we want to bring into our peaceful settlements a rough frontier population to violate the morals of our youth, overwhelm us by numbers and drive us again from our hard-earned homes." When the California gold rush reached its most frenzied moments in the summer of 1849, Brigham Young delivered this sermon in Salt Lake City:

"Do not any of you suffer the thought to enter your minds, that you must go to the gold mines in search of riches. That is no place for the Saints. Some have gone there and returned; they keep coming and going, but their garments are spotted, almost universally . . . . The man who is trying to gain for himself the perishable things of this world . . . may despair of ever obtaining a cross of glory."

Some Mormons in California and Nevada were active prospectors, but those in Utah heeded Young's words and did little or no mining. Instead the Mormons capital-ized on the needs of the miners in a way that aided their own growth without involving them in the distractions of the mining camps. Salt Lake City became a stopping-off point for easterners bound for California and Nevada; from 1849 on, the Mormons did a brisk business refitting travelers with equipment, selling them fresh horses, and supplying provisions. As a ring of mining camps appeared in the surrounding territories, Salt Lake City became an important trade center, providing food and freighting services for them. A network of railroads connected Salt Lake City with the mine areas by the 1860's. The Mormon capital also became a busy ore-processing center.

In the course of all this work the Mormons managed to keep Gentile settlers out of their region, and continued to practice their religion according to their special beliefs. One belief in particular brought them into conflict with the government: Since 1841, some Mormon men had been allowed to take several wives apiece. Joseph Smith had apparently had a number of wives, although this is not certain; but quite definitely Brigham Young had many wives, as did other leading members of the church. They argued that this practice, known as *polygamy*, could be justified by the Bible, since most of the Old Testament patriarchs had been polygamists. But polygamy seemed new and strange and shocking to most Americans, and the government passed a law prohibiting it. In 1862 a detachment of United States Army troops led by General Patrick E. Connor arrived in Utah Territory to see to it that the federal antipolygamy laws were being observed there.

General Connor disliked the Mormons, but with his slender force of seven hundred men was unable to make a serious challenge to their way of life. The well-trained Mormon militia stood ready to defend Salt Lake City against any government oppression. So the general chose a subtle way of trying to break Mormon control of Utah. He encouraged his men to prospect for gold, hoping to touch off a treasure-hunt that would fill Utah with thousands of Gentiles. These, he said, could "by peaceful means and through the ballot box . . . overwhelm the Mormons by force of numbers, and thus wrest from the church—disloyal and traitorous to the core—the absolute control of temporal and civic affairs."

In the summer of 1863 General Connor's troops discovered veins of lead, gold, and silver in Bingham Canyon, thirty miles south of Salt Lake City. Connor gave the discovery wide publicity, and a mining district was founded at Bingham Canyon by the end of the year. Though the precious metals there were mined out within a few decades, rich deposits of copper remained, and today the Kennecott Copper Company operates the world's biggest open-pit copper mine at what once was Bingham Canyon: a gigantic gash in the earth from which more than $2,000,000,000 worth of copper has been taken.

The prospectors who flocked to Bingham Canyon in the 1860's spread out over the rest of Utah in time, to the great dismay of the Mormons. But there was nothing they could do about it, short of erecting a wall around their territory. Despite the Mormon opposition to prospecting, therefore, Utah came to have a great many mining camps, most of which are ghost towns today.

One of the most interesting of these is Silver Reef, in the southwestern corner of the state, not far from Zion National Park. It takes its name from the one hundred-mile-long reef, as miners often call an ore-bearing rock formation, of silver-containing sandstone in this part of Utah. Geologists did not believe that silver could be found in sedimentary rock such as sandstone, but the geologists were wrong. A prospector named John Kemple, spending the winter of 1866-67 in that part of Utah, was roaming the area when he noticed what seemed to be an outcrop of silver in a sandstone vein. He succeeded in getting free a small knob of silver with his pick; but the lode did not look particularly promising, and he moved on to Nevada in the spring without attempting a deeper survey. For the next few years he brooded about the oddity of finding silver in sandstone, and in 1870 he and some friends returned to have another look. They camped on the reef, verified the richness of the lode, and organized a mining district.

There are several other versions of the discovery story. According to one, a wayfarer who stopped for the night at a house in the town of Leeds, near the sandstone reef, was standing by the fire when he spied some glittering drops oozing from the rocks lining the fireplace. He examined them and found them to be molten silver. The fireplace had been built of sandstone quarried from the nearby reef, and it was full of silver ore!

Another tale has it that miners in Pioche, Nevada, distrusted the accuracy of the local assayer, a man named Murphy. Murphy's assay reports were always much too optimistic; he seemed to find valuable ore in every rock sample. To test him, some of the Pioche miners bought a grindstone that a peddler from Utah was selling. They pulverized it and took a sample of the rock to Murphy, knowing that it was only worthless sandstone. True to form, Murphy reported an assay of two hundred ounces of silver to the ton. But before they could expose his "error," Murphy had traced the origin of the grindstone to the sandstone reef near Leeds, and was on his way to Utah to stake his claim.

A number of small mining camps sprang up along the reef, but it was impossible for the prospectors to get any financing for their work, since the San Francisco bankers refused to lend money on anything so fantastic as a silver mine in a sandstone reef. So for the first few years only sketchy work was done. But in 1875 a miner named William Tecumseh Barbee located a claim where rich silver lay so close to the surface of the sandstone that he needed no heavy equipment to mine it. Barbee set up a camp called Bonanza City and sent accounts of it to the Salt Lake *Tribune.* Early in 1876 he wrote that Bonanza City was "three weeks old and can boast an assay office, a blacksmith shop, a sampling works, a boarding house and several other wick-a-ups [shacks] of smaller dimensions, and will soon have a miners' supply store." On February 7, 1876, he declared in a letter to the paper, "This sandstone country beats all the boys, and it is amusing to see how excited they get when they go round to see the sheets of silver which are exposed all over the different reefs . . . . This is the most unfavorable looking country for mines that I have ever seen . . . but as the mines are here, what are the rock sharps going to do about it?"

By "the rock sharps" Barbee meant the geological experts of the Smithsonian Institution. One of the Bonanza City prospectors had sent the Smithsonian a piece of petrified wood from the site that was shot through with silver, and had received a polite reply referring to the sample as an "interesting fake as silver in nature is not formed in petrified wood." Nevertheless, this combination was quite common around Bonanza City.

Barbee was as good a press agent as he was a prospector, and his letters to the newspapers brought thousands of miners into the district—hardly any of them, of course, Mormons. Among those who came was a Nevada merchant named Hyrum Jacobs, who saw a chance for profit. He had his store transported in sections from Pioche, and assembled it right atop the reef, in the midst of the mining area. A camp took form around it, which in 1878 was incorporated as the city of Silver Reef. Gradually Silver Reef absorbed the adjoining camp of Bonanza City. Hyrum Jacobs next imported a stamp mill, machinery and all, from Bullionville, Nevada. It was the first mill to go into operation at Silver Reef.

The town thrived. A newspaper, the Silver Reef *Echo,* began publication in 1877; a brewery opened; a church, a hospital, and a school appeared. Although Silver Reef's streets remained unpaved for a long time, they were flanked by hotels and restaurants, stores, a bank, and a Wells Fargo office. A community center, Citizens Hall, was the site of Protestant services and Sunday School classes.

Silver Reef's population was nearly all Gentile, but there were a few Mormons, including the town's telegraph operator. Frequently, government agents would pass through Silver Reef on their way to make arrests in nearby St. George; a Mormon town where polygamy was common. The Silver Reef operator would give the warning by wiring a code message to the St. George telegraph office, which was in a furniture store, ordering "two chairs." Mormons and Gentiles got along fairly well in that part of Utah. Father Scanlan, Silver Reef's Catholic priest, became so popular among the Mormons of St. George that they invited him to celebrate Mass in their tabernacle, and the Mormon choir went to the trouble of learning Latin for the occasion, so it could provide the proper accompaniment.

No mining town's history would be complete without at least one devastating fire. Silver Reef's turn came in 1879, when a third of the business district burned down. The rest of the town was saved by a bucket brigade of men who filled empty powder kegs at the creek and passed them from hand to hand to douse the blaze. One restaurant was protected by its Chinese cook, who soaked its walls with milk.

Prosperity allowed Silver Reef to recover quickly. Such companies as the Leeds Silver Mining Company, the Barbee and Walker Mill and Mining Company, and the Stormont Silver Mining Company kept the mills going constantly. The financial side of western mining had changed a good deal during the 1870's; it was rare now for individual miners to work their own claims, except on an extremely small basis, and most of the mines were owned by large companies backed by capitalists from New York or San Francisco. Prospectors discovered mines, sold their claims to one of these companies, and went in search of new discoveries.

The profits of the Silver Reef mining companies were handsome. The Christy Mill and Mining Company milled some ten thousand tons of ore worth $302,000 in 1878, and by 1882 had recovered $1,275,000 worth of bullion from its sixteen mines. The Stormont Company and Barbee and Walker each produced a million dollars' worth of silver between 1878 and 1882. The Buckeye Mining Company was turning out a thousand-ounce brick of silver a day for a while.

Stockholders in these companies reaped fat dividends. But in 1881 troubles began. The price of silver dropped; some of the mines were invaded by underground streams; and the best ore deposits started to play out. Dividends were cut. Stockholders demanded that their profits be improved by cutting the wages of the miners. The mine operators announced that henceforth they would pay $3.50 a day instead of the standard wage of $4. The miners promptly formed a union and went on strike. For a month the mills of Silver Reef were silent. When sixty of the union men staged a demonstration, the sheriff formed a posse to arrest them, and they were imprisoned in a local dance hall, since the town jail was too small to hold that many. In disgust, most of the experienced miners left town for good. New men were hired to break the strike, but they were unfamiliar with the maze of shafts and tunnels under Silver Reef, and production dropped. A number of the mines closed down. The *Engineering and Mining Journal* commented early in 1884, "It would be difficult to imagine a more dull and lifeless mining camp than this place at the present time. The Barbee and Christy mills are both idle . . . . The Stormont continues running."

In 1891 the last of Silver Reef's mines ceased operations. In a period of little more than fifteen years, the sandstone reef had yielded some $10,000,000 in silver, but now all was quiet. A few local men leased the mines and between 1892 and 1903 took $250,000 worth of ore from them, but that was a far cry from the big days of 1877-80. Since then some half-hearted attempts to revive Silver Reef have come to nothing. A visitor who toured the town about 1950 reported:

> Today the racetrack is an alfalfa field, the cemetery is neglected, the blocks of wooden sidewalks have rotted away, and only adobe and stone walls line the rocky, sage-clogged streets. The stone bank is a summer home, its vault torn off and flower beds bordering the building; for the townsite is now private property, and a barbed-wire fence posted with "No Trespassing" signs surrounds the tract. Just inside the fence one large stone store, with iron shutters awry and dusty windowpanes, stands a glassy-eyed sentinel, brooding over the camp. . . .

North of Utah lies Idaho, which had a brief, wild mining boom of its own in the 1860's, and then settled down to steady, quiet production of minerals once the excitement over placer gold had ended. As early as the 1840's, Catholic missionaries had noticed gold in the streams of Idaho, but the hostility of the Indians had kept prospectors away. Idaho was the home of the fierce Nez Percé Indians, who tolerated no white trespassers.

In the summer of 1859 Captain E. D. Pierce, a trader

who had won the friendship of the Indians, washed gold from the bed of Canal Creek on Idaho's Clearwater River. By the following spring Idaho was full of prospectors. The Indians protested, but it was impossible for them to drive away the thousands of gold-seekers. Mining camps such as Oro Fino and Pierce City were founded and grew to populations of seven thousand and more within months.

Dozens of these camps were born and died, for, as the nineteenth-century historian H. H. Bancroft put it, "the miners of Idaho were like quicksilver," and "ran after any atom of gold in their vicinity." The roughest, toughest men from California, Nevada, and points west crowded into these camps, brawling and drinking and occasionally mining, and when the easy pickings were gone, they took off at once for the next discovery site. Typical of Idaho's numerous ghost towns is Silver City, whose bonanza days are far in the past.

Silver City was the most durable of a group of mining camps in Idaho's Owyhee Basin, west of Boise. A Canadian trader gave the Owyhee River its name in memory of two of his employees who were killed on its banks; they came from Hawaii, and that was the best job of spelling he could do. Supposedly emigrants bound for Oregon in 1847, before the days of the gold rush, had camped beside a creek in the Owyhee area and had picked some strange soft stones from the bed of the creek, pounding them flat and using them as sinkers for

their fishing lines. Only after the discovery at Sutter's Mill did they realize that the "stones" had been nuggets of gold.

In the spring of 1863 a band of thirty prospectors came out from the mining camp of Placerville, Idaho, which had been founded only a few months before. They panned in a number of the creeks running into the Owyhee, turned up plenty of "color" in the gravel, and staked claims before returning to Placerville. Soon the usual armies of prospectors were roaming the Owyhee country and forming mining camps. The town of Boonville was the first, but its location in a narrow canyon left no room for expansion, and soon the camp of Ruby City was laid out a mile up the creek in a better town site. The Boise *News* sent a reporter to Ruby City whose account appeared in the edition of June 4, 1864. He told of "whips popping, hammers knocking, planes planing, saws sawing, augers boring, anvils ringing, miners singing, horses running, (with fellows on 'em), and bull-drivers swearing . . . . The Pony Express made two successful trips from Humboldt to Ruby City bringing San Francisco papers only seven days old . . . . Horseback riding is a favorite pastime with ladies and gents of Owyhee . . . . Owyhee is a gay place. About the only seedy individuals are the lawyers."

By the end of 1864 Ruby City had a population of one thousand and had been designated the county seat

of newly formed Owyhee County. But it had a powerful rival in Silver City, which had been founded late in
1863 one mile farther up the creek. Silver City was
closer to the mines than Ruby City, and its snug location in a high valley protected it from the harsh winds
that raked the older town. Gradually Ruby City was
engulfed by her rival. The inhabitants of Ruby City
moved to Silver City, and many of Ruby City's buildings were hauled to new sites in the other town. Even
the Owyhee *Avalanche,* the district's first newspaper,
joined the exodus. Founded in Ruby City on August 19,
1865, the *Avalanche* shifted its office to Silver City
exactly twelve months later. In 1866 Silver City became the new county seat and the eclipse of Ruby City
was complete.

During 1863 and 1864 most of the mining along
Jordan Creek, where Silver City and her neighbors
were located, was placer mining. But this work, though
profitable at first, was soon abandoned to the Chinese,
who patiently continued to wash gravel that the white
settlers scorned to touch. By 1864 most of the miners
were at work in the rich quartz veins of nearby War
Eagle Mountain. The first mine found there assayed
$7,000 in silver and $800 in gold to the ton, and the
rock could be pounded up in hand mortars, so costly mills
were unnecessary. That mine yielded $2,750,000 in six
years.

Silver City's most productive mine was called the

Poorman. Two miners, named Hays and Ray, staked the first claim in 1865, but did not try to develop the vein. A little while later a man named C. S. Peck noticed an ore outcropping in the same region. He found that the vein was on the Hays-Ray claim, and without telling them of his find he offered to buy the mine. The price they quoted was more than he was willing to pay, and he withdrew to consider the matter. Meanwhile other prospectors rediscovered the Peck vein, staked a claim, and named the mine the Poorman. Hays and Ray pointed out that the claim overlapped their own. But the owners of the Poorman claim controlled the best approach to the ore; they erected a fort at the mouth of the mine and posted armed guards there while waiting for the assayer's report. The report was enthusiastic, and a lawsuit to determine the rightful owner of the mine seemed certain—but the quarrel was settled peacefully when both sets of claimants agreed to sell out to a third group. Between 1866 and 1875 the Poorman produced $4,000,000 of silver; its easily worked ore assayed better than $4,000 to the ton.

A boundary dispute involving ownership of the Golden Chariot and the Ida Elmore mines was not settled so peacefully. During a feud concerning overlapping claims, both sides hired gunmen, and the owner of the Ida Elmore was killed in a battle that lasted three days. At last the government authorities in Boise had to send cavalry to restore order.

The miners, too, battled for their rights. In 1872 the three hundred miners of the Mahogany mine protested the harsh treatment they were receiving at the hands of the mine foreman, John Jewell. They demanded Jewell's removal. When the mine superintendent refused to dismiss the foreman, the miners became unruly, and the superintendent ordered forty armed men and two small cannons into duty to keep them under control. This touched off a protest strike involving four adjoining mines, whose miners said they would do no work as long as Jewell kept his job. The unpopular foreman was discharged.

Though occasionally harassed by unfriendly Indians, Silver City grew steadily. One of its first big buildings was the Idaho Hotel, a frame structure originally built in Ruby City and hauled in three sections to Jordan Street in the new town. Still in existence, though unoccupied for years and somewhat the worse for wear, the Idaho Hotel had fifty guest rooms and a handsome dining room in the basement. Wells Fargo rented part of the hotel as a shipping office until its own building, just to the south, was constructed. Outside the Wells Fargo office stacks of silver bars used to stand until picked up by stagecoach drivers for shipment to San Francisco. Next door was the office of the Owyhee *Avalanche*, which was published for nearly seventy years. The yellowed pages of its files reveal such stories as these:

[October 28, 1865] Mr. Cox recently of Silver City, was killed by Indians on Wed. morning. Himself and family were moving in a wagon to Boise City, and when just beyond the summit, between Reynolds' Creek and the Snake River, they were fired on and Mr. Cox instantly killed. His wife drove on rapidly and escaped.

[January 27, 1866] The Owyhee Debating Club meets every Thursday evening in the Sheriff's office. The subject of this week was, "Resolved, That the immigration of the Mongolian race to this Coast should be prohibited by law." It was decided in the negative.

[February 3, 1866] According to an old woman's saying that "bread is the staff of life, but whisky is life itself" we are out of "life" just now, though there is flour enough to meet present needs.

[June 1, 1867] The contract for building a Court House and Jail for Owyhee County was let last Wednesday. The jail is to be 30 feet by 22 feet, running back into the hill, built of hewn lumber set on end and lined with two inch planks spiked on; floors and ceilings to be of hewn timber. The Courthouse will be of two stories on top of the jail, running back ten feet farther into the hill. . . . The first floor will contain offices for the county officers, lined and papered. The upper story will contain three rooms—the Courtroom, the District Clerk's office and a jury room.

Only the shell of the courthouse remains. Its upper stories and interior are gone, but the stone arches of its façade are still in place. A block from the courthouse is a two-story frame house, all that is left of the War

Eagle Hotel. When Silver City lived, the War Eagle was an assortment of miscellaneous buildings of varying heights and shapes, lined up along Washington Street, but its annexes all have vanished. Not far away is the Masonic lodge, built in 1865. Since the lodge spanned Jordan Creek, Silver City's Masons were fond of entering the building by the front door, leaving it by the back, and declaring that they had just "crossed the Jordan." The Chinese, who rarely tried to mingle socially with the white inhabitants of a mining town, had their own Masonic lodge. On the far side of the creek, looking down on the business section, stands one of Silver City's youngest buildings, a church. It was built by Episcopalians in 1896, and when no Episcopalians remained by 1933 it was sold to the Catholics.

By 1870 Idaho's first mining boom was over. The Wells Fargo agent in Boise estimated the 1869 production of gold and silver in the territory at $8,000,000, and the 1870 output at only $6,000,000. Thereafter the trend continued downward. But the Idaho gold rush had served to bring settlers into an unpeopled region of great fertility. "As the placer mines decline," said the Boise *Statesman* on July 1, 1870, "persons forsake them for the more permanent pursuits of farming and stock-breeding . . . the grain, hay and vegetable crop of Boise and other agricultural districts is better than ever." Silver City continued to produce steadily while output was dipping elsewhere, but by 1873 most of its mines had shut down. The ore was still there for the taking, but a financial panic in San Francisco had disrupted the mining industry, and without a flow of capital from San Francisco investors it was impossible to develop and maintain the inland mines.

There was a slow revival as local investors took the place of the San Francisco capitalists. The Owyhee *Avalanche* printed an advertisement in February 1875 under the heading, "Miners Wanted," which called for "twenty good miners" to work in the revived War Eagle mine, and added, "It is estimated that fully 1000 additional men will be needed this spring to work the mines of this camp." The pay offered was "$4 in coin per day."

In the 1880's Silver City was vigorous again; new mines were opened and old ones were expanded. The *Avalanche* acquired the first telegraphic news wire in the Idaho Territory, to keep its readers abreast of national and world developments. New buildings went up, including a brewery that offered "Owyhee Beer." But in the twentieth century the mines became exhausted, and the last of them was closed for good in 1942. A year later Silver City's post office and telephone services were discontinued, making it an official ghost town. But in 1948 the main access route was improved, and members of the Kiwanis Club of Payette, Idaho, posted labels on the historic buildings. Since then the old town has become a favorite attraction for tourists.

Wyoming's gold rush also began in the 1860's. The first discoveries were made in central Wyoming, high in the Wind River Mountains, near the present town of Lander. This is a region of rugged peaks more than 10,000 feet above sea level, which created formidable barriers for the emigrants heading to Oregon in the first wave of westward settlement. The chief route through the mountains was South Pass, 7,500 feet above sea level. South Pass was discovered early in the nineteenth century; missionaries and fur traders used it in the 1830's, and a decade later hundreds of ox-drawn wagons plodded through it. Brigham Young led his Mormons to Utah via South Pass in 1847. As early as 1842, a fur trader discovered placer gold in the Sweetwater River, which runs through South Pass, but he was killed by Indians, it seems, before he could take advantage of his find. Thirteen years later prospectors did some work along the Sweetwater, but their profits were not great enough to start a stampede into this desolate, difficult-to-reach area where marauding Indians made life risky. Now and then some bold individual would do a little free-lance placer mining on the Sweetwater, but no boom developed until government troops started patrolling the region in the summer of 1866. Some of the soldiers had been miners in California and Nevada, and they quickly detected the outcroppings of gold-bearing quartz. A few months later, when their military service was over, they returned to South Pass as prospectors.

Indians drove them away, but not before they had confirmed their original hunches about the geology of the Sweetwater Valley.

In June 1867 a party of prospectors rediscovered the lode seen by the soldiers the year before. They set to work with pick and drill, ignoring the dangers of Indian attack, and were busily extracting the gold-bearing quartz when an Indian war party arrived. One of the miners was killed and several were wounded; the Indians stole their horses, leaving the men to stumble back on foot to the nearest military outpost, Fort Bridger. They armed themselves and returned to the lode, keeping their guns beside them as they dug, and posting a sentry atop a hill.

As in Idaho, Indian opposition melted before a sud-

den influx of prospectors. Seven hundred miners were at work in South Pass by the fall of 1867. They staked claims, built log cabins with dirt floors and sod roofs, and organized a town called South Pass City. As the fierce winter closed in, they stockpiled great quantities of wood for fuel, stored away the meat of elk, buffalo, and deer, and spent the winter months crushing in hand mortars the ore they had mined earlier. South Pass was then part of Dakota Territory, and in January 1868, the territorial legislature of Dakota approved the creation of Carter County; South Pass City became the county seat the following year.

By the end of 1868 there were four thousand residents. The city had five hotels, three meat markets, four law firms, and thirteen saloons. It was a big year for mining, too. Every gulch for ten miles around proved to contain gold. New camps, themselves ghost towns today, were founded nearby: Atlantic City, four miles away, and Miners' Delight, four miles farther on. But South Pass City remained the most important town of the area. Its big mine, the Carissa, reached a depth of four hundred feet in 1868; pumping machinery, a steam hoist, and a six-stamp mill were installed.

Indian harassment was a perpetual problem. The Indians were unable to deal with the intruders in a direct confrontation, but they hovered at the edges of the settlement, trying to pick off stragglers who got too far from town. Hardly a month went by without a victim. A freight driver called Uncle Ben Hurst, carrying a load of goods to South Pass City with his four-ox team, was attacked by Indians on his way to town. They wounded his assistant seriously; Hurst was able to drive them off, and left his companion under the wagon, wrapped in blankets and barricaded behind rocks, while he drove to South Pass to get help. When he returned with a posse, he found that the Indians had come back, killed the man, and cleaned out the goods on the wagon. The posse itself encountered an Indian raiding party as it headed toward South Pass, and one man was killed. A few months later, in September 1869, Sioux raiders near Miners' Delight slew a man who was hauling lime, and ran off with his team of oxen. Then they crossed to Atlantic City and killed a man chopping wood there. The South Pass *News* devoted its issue of April 9, 1870, to "The Indian Outrages" and complained of "the recent murders committed by Indians upon numbers of our peaceful citizens." The general attitude in South Pass City was that the Indians, having lost their land to the white invaders, were acting treacherously by refusing to settle down politely on the reservations that had been allotted them. The miners could not understand why the Indians declined to accept the situation.

Under the circumstances, the only way to keep order was to kill the troublesome savages. The territorial governor sent an army colonel to South Pass to organize a militia; but the officer and his men lost enthusiasm when they were informed that it was against government policy for them to commence a wholesale massacre of the Indians.

One pioneer settler in South Pass remarked many years later that "Firearms were needed in self-defense against whites as well as Indians." Dr. George A. Carpenter, writing in 1934, recalled, "The man I worked for was slain from ambush one night just outside my shack on Rock Creek. Everyone knew who did it. The killer was taken before a justice of the peace. He raised his right hand and swore innocence. That was all. He was freed."

South Pass City made Dakota political history in 1869. Mrs. Esther Morris, one of the town's leading citizens, was a suffragette—a woman who believed that those of her sex should have the right to vote, something that was denied women in nineteenth-century America. She gave a tea party at her home for the Republican and Democratic candidates for the territorial legislature and got each of them to pledge that if elected he would introduce a bill giving women the vote. The Republican, W. H. Bright, won the election and persuaded the legislature to pass Mrs. Morris' bill. Not only did the women of Dakota receive the vote, they were now permitted to hold office as well, and South Pass City promptly elected Mrs. Morris justice of the peace.

At first the tougher men in town rebelled at the thought of a female judge, but she succeeded in establishing her authority, and handled the forty cases that were brought before her with fairness and skill.

The boom in South Pass City reached its climax by 1872. It was the second largest city in Dakota Territory then, and its lively main street ran for half a mile along the gulch. Then the placer deposits gave out, and about the same time the deeper lodes proved difficult to work. When gold was discovered to the east in 1874, much of the population moved away. In that year a military expedition led by General George A. Custer struck gold in the Black Hills of Dakota. Custer, whose tragic last stand against Sioux warriors lay less than two years in the future, had been exploring the Black Hills with the Seventh U.S. Cavalry when his men found gold in a creek three and a half miles from the present town of Custer, South Dakota. He tried to keep the find a secret until he had had a chance to file a report with Washington, but somehow it leaked out, and the Chicago *Inter Ocean* printed the story on August 27, 1874, under these headlines:

GOLD!!
THE LAND OF PROMISE
Stirring News From the
Black Hills

THE GLITTERING TREASURE
Found At Last—a Belt
Of Gold Territory
30 Miles Wide
THE PRECIOUS DUST
Found Under The
Horses' Feet
EXCITEMENT
Among the Troops

Soon the Chicago newspaper's great scoop was being reprinted far and wide, and the Black Hills gold rush was on. By 1875 the town of Deadwood, South Dakota, was taking form—a wild, boisterous mining camp that soon included in its large population such celebrated western characters as Wild Bill Hickok (who was murdered there in 1876) and Calamity Jane. By the middle of July 1876, Deadwood had 25,000 inhabitants or perhaps more; as one of them wrote, "You can't count people who are living in layers." The rush to the Black Hills cleaned out many of the mining camps to the west, and turned South Pass City into a ghost town.

South Pass City never recovered. By 1878 the place was nearly abandoned; grass grew in the streets, and the mines were silent. In 1885 the Carissa mine was reopened and worked for a while, but no great stampede back to South Pass developed. Not even the discovery of a large ore body in the 1890's aroused much enthusiasm. A new mill opened, and the population of the town increased by fifty or a hundred, but most of its weather-beaten cabins and aging stores stayed empty. A little excitement developed in the summer of 1933 when a dredging operation began in the old placer fields. Dredging is mining carried out from a flat-bottomed boat that floats on an artificial pond; the pond is created by damming the stream where the dredging is to be done. The dredge bites into the earth, scooping up buckets of dirt and moving them along a conveyer chain to machinery that separates gold from waste. Another chain-and-bucket arrangement in the rear of the dredge disposes of the waste, so as the dredge moves along it leaves behind a series of immense piles of rock and earth, which remain bare and ugly for years until finally covered by vegetation. When the dredging began at South Pass, a Wyoming newspaper declared:

HUNDREDS NOW IN SOUTH PASS HUNTING GOLD
PRESENT REVIVAL MAY ECLIPSE PAST PEAK
That the ghost mining cities of Atlantic City and South Pass at the crest of the Continental Divide in Fremont County are heading to a revival that will eclipse the palmy days of the region when Miners' Delight and other million dollar operations, with but crude equipment turned out hundreds of thousands of dollars in yellow metal and contributed to two of the wildest mining camps of the early days, is seen in present activities at several modernly equipped

plants, where showings of heavy gold recovery both in lode and placer mining have been attracting the attention of hundreds of people who visit the district daily.

The revival of South Pass City was only a flash in the pan. The dredges went away, leaving the shabby, time-worn city further disfigured by the great dredge dumps. Today the town clings to life with a population of about one hundred; a few of the boom-time stores and other buildings survive, but South Pass City has little left but glowing memories. Deadwood, the city that drained away most of Wyoming's prospectors, has come through the decades in much better condition. No ghost town at all, Deadwood has a population of several thousand; mines are still being worked a few miles away, while in the downtown section the streets of the 1870's are carefully preserved and attract platoons of visitors every year.

NINE
Montana's Lawless Camps

THE MINING CAMPS of the West mostly have reputations for lawlessness, brutality, and general disorder. Lynchings, bank robberies, stagecoach holdups, gun duels on Main Street, and all the rest, so familiar from movies and television, supposedly were standard daily fare in the old towns. There was no law except the law of the gun, and virtuous citizens cowered under their beds while the gunslingers shot up the town.

A lot of this is pure myth. The seamy reputations of some places were invented long after the fact by shrewd promoters trying to gain a "Wild West" image that would draw tourists to their town. While no western town was precisely a model of polite behavior, there was less feuding and slaughtering than we have come to believe. The miners were tough, aggressive men whose interests occasionally clashed, and there was plenty of gunplay, particularly when gambling debts or women were involved. But such episodes were usually well spaced, and most of the time the prospectors went about their business in a reasonably law-abiding way, deciding the majority of disputes through improvised courts and not with their guns.

One place where most of the legends of lawlessness are true, though, is Montana. The gold rush that convulsed Montana began early in the 1860's, more or less at the same time that the Idaho, Utah, and Wyoming stampedes were beginning. But for some reason Montana tended to attract men who had had no luck in the neighboring states, and some who had been floating around for ten or fifteen years or more with nothing to show for their adventures on the mining frontier. Into Montana's camps poured the dregs of the West— the desperadoes, the bandits, the brawlers. The mountainous western half of the state gave rise to some of the toughest towns of the boom days.

A half-breed named François Finlay, who usually went by his Indian name of Be-net-see, panned some gold in Montana as early as 1852 at the mouth of a tiny creek emptying into Deer Lodge River. Six years later two prospectors rediscovered this creek and confirmed the presence of gold in it. But that year attention was turning to Nevada and Colorado. Montana, which was then the eastern section of the Oregon Territory, did not receive serious exploration until 1862.

In the summer of that year a party of prospectors came through wild, untamed Montana from the east, hoping to find wealth in the Idaho gold camps. Before they reached Idaho they got word that pickings were lean there, since many thousands of miners were already at work, and so they halted in Montana. Moving through the Deer Lodge Valley, they camped on Grasshopper Creek and unpacked their placer pans. On July 28, 1862, John White and William Eads spied "color" in the creek.

A new boom was born. A second party of prospectors heading for Idaho from Colorado was deflected to the east by the rumors, and ended up in the new camp of Grasshopper Diggings. A group of Oregon-bound settlers from St. Paul happened to be passing through, and half of them forgot all about their plans to raise wheat, staying behind to pan for gold in Grasshopper Creek. By the end of 1862 Grasshopper Diggings had a population of five hundred.

As the town grew it acquired a new name: Bannack, after the tribe of Indians living in the vicinity. "Life in Bannack at this time was perfect isolation from the rest of the world," wrote Nathaniel Langford, a New Englander who was among its first residents. "All the great battles of the season of 1862—Antietam, Fredericksburg, Second Bull Run—all the exciting debates of Congress, and the more exciting battles at sea, first became known to us on the arrival of the newspapers in the spring of 1863." Another Montanan observed of Bannack in 1863, "It was not supposed to be a settlement, but simply a mining camp where everyone was trying to get what he could, and then go home."

Placer mining quickly was followed by lode mining. Bannack's Dakota mine was opened in 1862; it had a six-stamp mill driven by water power. Soon there were other deep mines open, and the hills above Grasshopper Creek were pockmarked with the dumping of mine waste. Gold was abundant, and the only thing that kept Bannack from becoming a real metropolis was the discovery in 1863 of an even richer group of mines at Alder Gulch, not far to the east. Many of Bannack's fickle inhabitants scurried across the hills to the new bonanza camps that were springing up at Alder Gulch.

Enough stayed at Bannack, though, to give the town a certain political importance. In 1863 the Oregon Territory was carved up, with Idaho, Montana, and Wyoming cut out of it and placed in the newly created Idaho Territory. In September of that year, Bannack was visited by Sidney Edgerton, who was on his way to take up residence in Lewiston, Idaho, as chief justice of Idaho Territory. The judge did not care to risk the mountain journey westward in the winter, so he spent the next few months in Bannack. In the spring he recommended to Congress that Idaho Territory be further divided, and on May 26, 1864, Congress passed the law bringing Montana Territory into existence. Bannack, which had been in Oregon, Idaho, and now Montana all within two years, was picked as the temporary capital of the new territory, and Edgerton was chosen the first governor of Montana. A red brick building was erected in Bannack to serve as the territorial capitol. The first legislative assembly of Montana held its initial meeting there on December 12, 1864. Soon after, however, Bannack lost her lofty position to a faster-growing city in Alder Gulch, and the first meeting of the legislature in the new capitol building was also its last.

Though Bannack had the glory of being a territorial capital for a little while, it also had the doubtful distinction of sheltering one of the West's most sinister criminals: the dreaded Henry Plummer. Plummer was a road agent—that is, a bandit who preyed on stagecoaches carrying gold and passengers from town to town—who terrorized much of the West before his career came to an end in Bannack.

He learned his grim trade in California, and in the spring of 1861 moved east to Idaho. He showed up in the important river town of Lewiston, accompanied by a wife (whom he soon deserted) and booked a room in the best hotel. Quietly and giving no hint of his true profession, Plummer organized a criminal network operating out of Lewiston. He set up two "shebangs," or roadside inns, along the main highways, one controlling the route to the gold fields east of Lewiston, the other monitoring the road west to Walla Walla. Each she-bang was staffed by a couple of Plummer's henchmen. Plummer himself remained in Lewiston, observing the movements of miners and bullion. When he found a likely victim, he sent word to one of his shebangs to intercept the shipment.

Plummer would manage to learn all about the horses making up each pack train carrying gold out of Lewis-

ton: the number of horses, their color, brand, style of saddle, and date of purchase. Then he would draw up counterfeit bills of sale showing one of his shebang-keepers as the legal owner of the animals. When the pack train reached the shebang, Plummer's men would produce these bills of sale and demand the horses, taking the precious cargo as well. Few of the pack train drivers cared to argue the point, especially with guns aimed at their heads.

In the spring of 1862 Plummer's activities were arousing suspicion in Lewiston and he began to look for a new base of operations. When he heard about the Grasshopper Creek discoveries that summer, he chose Bannack for his headquarters. The day he arrived he shot a man to death. Brought to trial before a jury of miners, Plummer served as his own lawyer and spoke so eloquently that he was acquitted on grounds of self-defense. Plummer seemed so virtuous, in fact, that the citizens of Bannack elected him sheriff.

Sheriff Plummer kept the law by day and trampled on it by night. He collected an assortment of cutthroats, highwaymen, and miscellaneous fugitives from justice who had drifted into Montana's gold fields, and organized them into an efficient gang of road agents operating on the ninety-mile stretch of highway between Bannack and Alder Gulch. A string of rest stops for stagecoaches lined this road, and at each of these stations was one of Plummer's men, keeping an eye on the passing traffic. Whenever a stagecoach laden with gold went through, word was sent ahead and the gang gathered to pounce on it. Usually the shipper of the gold informed the sheriff in advance of the departure of the cargo, so that he could give it special protection —and Plummer, of course, took full advantage of this situation.

For more than a year the Plummer bandits dominated the road, looting nearly every gold shipment, killing more than a hundred men, and making the region around Bannack the most lawless in the land. The miners, desperate to find some way to get their gold safely to civilization, resorted to ingenious devices such as secret compartments in their wagons. But still the raids continued, while Sheriff Plummer piously announced that he was doing his best to end the shameful state of affairs. Now and then some bandit was seized and thrust into the Bannack jail, a small wooden building with a sod roof, said to have been built by Plummer himself, but convictions were rarities. Sometimes angry citizens formed vigilante committees and took the law into their own hands; some of Plummer's men were captured this way, although no one yet realized that the sheriff himself was directing the crime wave. Among those caught was George Shears, one of Plummer's lieutenants. The posse rigged a gallows for him at Hell Gate Store, Montana, and asked him to walk up a ladder to save them the trouble of preparing a drop for him. "Gentlemen," said Shears, "I am not used to this business. Shall I jump off or slide off?" He was told to jump.

Plummer approved of this vigilante action. In January 1864, he entertained a group of important citizens in his Bannack home, including the territorial governor and some of the leading vigilantes, and spoke favorably of their efforts to stamp out the banditry. A few days later he took part in a holdup himself, masked and gloved. Rashly he removed his gloves to carry the sacks of bullion from the stagecoach, and one of the passengers recognized Plummer's hands. Shortly thereafter the sheriff was arrested, tried, condemned, and, with two of his deputies, hanged on January 10, 1864.

The gallows at Hangman's Gulch where Plummer died has been reconstructed by Bannack for the benefit of visitors. Plummer remained cool until the noose was about to go around his neck; then he begged to be spared. "I am too wicked to die," he said. "Cut off my ears, strip me naked and let me go, but spare my life." The townsfolk persisted in their desire to dispose of him, though, and he grew calm again. "As a last favor, gentlemen, let me beg that you will give me a good drop," he declared.

Bannack, after Plummer's execution, was a quieter place. The worst criminals were gone, and so, it appeared, was the gold. In 1864 and 1865 mining came nearly to a halt, despite the completion in 1864 of a large steam-operated stamp mill costing $25,000. Most of the local activity had shifted to Alder Gulch. But in 1866 two Bannack prospectors built a ditch to bring in water from an adjoining creek; this made placer mining much simpler at Bannack, where the low level of Grasshopper Creek had hampered work. Soon after, the Bannack Mining and Ditch Company constructed a thirty-mile canal at a cost of $35,000, and by 1870 three more canals were feeding water to the town. A decade or so of fairly active placer mining followed. Then the local gravel was totally exhausted of gold, and when the "color" no longer showed, Bannack slid into ghostliness.

In 1895, after the invention of the electric gold dredge, the slumbering town awakened. The first dredging operation came up with $40,000 worth of gold in two weeks. Before long, three more dredges were at work in the vicinity, and these virtually cleaned out all that remained. A couple of the deep mines remained open until about 1914, but the population never got much beyond one hundred or so. The Bannack post office was closed in 1938. Today the town is all but silent, though it has a few patriotic inhabitants. Plummer's little jail still stands, as does the abandoned red brick building that was Montana's first territorial capitol, as well as some cabins, stores, and taverns, nearly all of them boarded up. There is little trace of the gaudy epoch of the Plummer gang, when Bannack's mines were busy and the town thrived.

Time has been more kind to the town that drained much of the vitality from Bannack: Virginia City, in Alder Gulch. Some miners out of Bannack discovered the gold of Alder Gulch in the spring of 1863, when hostile Indians forced them to cancel a prospecting trip to Yellowstone Valley. Henry Edgar, Bill Fairweather, and a few others dipped their pans in a creek bordered by alder bushes, came up with the rich glint of gold on May 26, and rushed back to Bannack for mining equipment and supplies. They tried to keep their find a secret, but it was obvious from their excitement and from the pattern of their purchases that they had found something big, and when they set out from Bannack again they were trailed by a mob of hopeful comrades, who soon were staking their own claims in Alder Gulch.

A string of mining camps appeared in the gulch. Most of them have long since vanished without a trace; one, Nevada City, survives only as half a dozen dilapidated shacks. Late in 1863 it was a flourishing boom town, its single street busy with stores, hotels, and cargo offices. The first of Plummer's men to be caught was executed at Nevada City: George Ives, who had killed a man named Nicholas Tiebalt and buried his body in Alder Gulch. When one of the locals reported hearing a shot and seeing a stranger drive off with Tiebalt's mules, a posse of twenty-five men searched the area and found Ives without much difficulty. They were bringing him back to Nevada City for trial when the bandit casually offered to wager that his horse could outrun all of theirs. The unsuspecting men of the posse took the bet, where-upon Ives spurred his mount and took off for the hills. He had disappeared before the posse realized that the "bet" was simply a ruse to cover Ives' escape.

Within two hours Ives was a prisoner again, and the vigilantes took no further chances with him. A jury of twenty-four men debated his fate by the light of a bonfire that night and speedily sentenced him to death. A small group of Plummer's men watched the execution, unable to save Ives as he went to his hanging.

Nevada City was short-lived, but just to the east in Alder Gulch rose the town of Virginia City, where in the first year of placer mining some $10,000,000 in gold was taken from a thousand claims. According to one tale, Virginia City, Montana, was named in honor of the more famous Virginia City then causing such a sensation in Nevada; but another account has it that when the new camp needed a name, one southern-born miner suggested "Varina City," in homage to the wife of Jefferson Davis, leader of the Confederacy. The patriotic northerners in the camp would not agree to this, and in a compromise the name of "Virginia City" was chosen. Virginia City was officially incorporated in January 1864, and soon was growing mightily at the expense of Bannack and the surrounding towns. A newspaper, the Montana *Post*, went into operation on August 27, 1864, putting out an edition of nine hundred sixty copies that quickly sold out even at the high price of fifty cents for the single sheet. The first issue offered this description of the new town:

> On arriving at this place what astonishes any stranger is the size, appearance and vast amount of business that is here beheld. Though our city is but a year old, fine and substantial buildings have been erected, and others are rapidly going up. One hundred buildings are being erected each week in Virginia City and environs . . . . Indeed the whole appears to be the work of magic— the vision of a dream. But Virginia City is not a myth, a paper town, but a reality . . . . The placer diggings will require years to work out . . . . Many persons are taking out $150 per day to the hand . . . . Wages are high, $6 to $12 per day. Old miners have the preference as they are worth much more than green hands . . . . The other side of the picture is this—we desire not to deceive, but to give facts. All the claims, as a matter of course, around our city, have long since been taken up. These must be purchased, and that too at very high figures. A "pilgrim" must work for somebody else or purchase a claim, or strike out for other diggings . . . .

Among the pilgrims who settled in Virginia City was a light-fingered young man from the East named James Knox Polk Miller, who sometimes found it convenient to go under the alias of "J. Sidney Osborn." Miller had been in business in New York in partnership with his uncle; in 1864, at the age of twenty, he pocketed $3,500 of his uncle's money and headed for the wide-open spaces. His first stop was Salt Lake City, where he opened a cigar shop. That was an unfortunate enterprise, since Salt Lake City was almost entirely populated by Mormons, whose religion forbade them to smoke. When he realized that he could not earn a living dealing only with his few fellow Gentiles, Miller moved on to Montana Territory, reaching Virginia City on June 6, 1865, just after his twenty-first birthday.

What he found was somewhat less glamorous than the Montana *Post* had described. He noted in his diary on June 7, "From Nevada's [Nevada City] west end to the east end of Virginia City is about 3 miles. The houses and stores are mostly on one street and are built of loggs, mud and stones with dirt roofs. The street runs along 'Virginia Gulch' where, for a width of 500 to 1000 feet, shovelled, uplifted & piled, it looks as if an enormous Hog had been uprooting the soil. My board and lodging at the Missouri House are to cost me $14 pr. week." That was a great deal of money for 1865, but, as the *Post* noted, "The abundance of gold mines makes everything high."

Miller had grown accustomed to the pious life of Salt Lake City, and his first Sunday in Virginia City, June 11, 1865, startled him. He wrote, "There was nothing visible to remind a person in any degree that it was Sunday. Every store, saloon and dancing hall was in full-blast. Hack running, auctioneering, mining, and indeed every business, is carried on with much more

zeal than on week days. It made me heartsick to see it."
However, although a church was available for the de-
vout, Miller offered up no prayers himself that day.
The Keystone Gymnastic Troupe was performing at
the Montana Theater, and he was asked to serve as
ticket-taker. "I spent the evening at the Montana Theater," he admitted to his diary. "Today showed me an
entirely new phase of life."

He did not plan to work as a miner, since, as the *Post*
had observed, all the claims were taken and the best he
could hope for was a job digging up gold for someone
else. He preferred less strenuous work. Since he had
arrived in Virginia City with just $2 left of his original
$3,500, he had to find a job quickly, and he signed up
as a bookkeeper. The pay was low, the cost of living
was enormous, and on June 8, 1866, he wrote gloomily
that he was "$5 worse off than nothing, after a year's
work in such a country as this, $3,500 worse off than
when I left the states. I much doubt whether the Lord
ever intends to let me make another 'Pile.' " Ten days
later he carried off ·a successful business deal, though,
netting $563.14 in a speculation in salt, and nothing
stopped him thereafter. He took French lessons, toyed
with the idea of enrolling at Princeton, visited St. Louis
to attend the theater, and in the summer of 1867 set sail
from New York to spend some of his savings on a tour
that took him through Europe to Egypt and the Holy
Land. After a year he was back in Montana, running a

successful store at Deer Lodge; in 1876 he moved to Deadwood, South Dakota, to cash in on the Black Hills gold rush, and went first into the real estate business, then became president of the Deadwood Central Railroad Company. Never in his western career did he stake a claim or pan for gold, yet he was a rich man when he died of tuberculosis in California in 1891, at the age of forty-six.

Virginia City's early career was as brilliantly successful as that of James Knox Polk Miller. The pages of the Montana *Post* convey the vigor of the town. The newspaper, which boasted in its first issue that "The latest telegraphic news will be given up to the time of going to press, so that our readers may be aware of what is passing in the outer world," did run a column on events elsewhere, quaintly headed "News from America," but its chief concern was local happenings. The edition of September 3, 1864, announced a prize fight "Between Riley of Virginia City and Foster of Bannack . . . . The men are under heavy training. We see by the cards of admission that no weapons of any kind are allowed around or outside the enclosure." The same issue published an advertisement declaring, "William Fairweather lost last week in Virginia City a valuable nugget of gold, being the first taken out of Virginia Gulch. The finder will be amply rewarded." Since fire was always a threat, the *Post*, on October 29, 1864, called for the institution of a nightly fire patrol: "One good, sober, vigilant man could be found to patrol from sun to sun, over all the town, and to give the alarm of fire. . . ." The fire patrol was duly organized, and the newspaper's editorialist turned his efforts next to the town's water supply. "Let someone look to the WATER," said the *Post* on November 12, 1864:

> The most important additions to the tools of a fire company, without an engine are two or three troughs holding about a barrel of water each. Such a trough laid on the ground and worked by a stout fellow throwing up water with a large wooden shovel, can do more than twelve bucket men—the direction, quickness and amount delivered being all on the side of the shovel.
>
> A good man can throw water with it on top of almost any house in town, except the two story buildings and the side walls of these can be kept safe by water thrown from the ground, where no man can stand the heat and smoke on a ladder.

By the end of 1864, reservoirs above the town were supplying water in wooden tubs at a price of $2 per month per family. Also opening that December was the Montana Theater, where James Knox Polk Miller would be tempted from virtue on a sunny Sunday six months later. The theater's first play was *Faint Heart Never Won Fair Lady*, followed by "'comic and sentimental songs," and a "roaring farce, *The Spectre Bridegroom*."

Virginia City also boasted a lecture hall, an assortment

of hotels, a Wells Fargo office, and many other flourishing places of business. There were numerous laundries,
operated, as always, by Chinese, who after washing the
clothes of the miners panned the wash water for gold
dust and turned a good profit. When Virginia City's
population reached ten thousand at the beginning of
1865, the territorial legislature voted to transfer the
capital there from Bannack, and Governor Edgerton
moved his official residence. Yet only a week or so after
Virginia City became the capital on February 7, 1865,
gossip had it that Virginia City was doomed to dwindle
as Bannack had. New gold mines had been found in the
Prickly Pear Valley to the north, and it was predicted that
most of Virginia's City's inhabitants would strike out
after the latest bonanza.

The prediction came true, but not right away. A
mining camp called Last Chance Gulch was founded
in the Prickly Pear Valley, and for a few years it paid
well. Its gold ran out by 1868, but silver, copper, and
other metals were found there. Last Chance Gulch
changed its name to Helena and ultimately replaced
Virginia City as the capital of Montana; but Virginia
City had plenty of good years left before it finally was
eclipsed by its competitor to the north.

During its early years Virginia City, like neighboring
Bannack, was plagued by lawlessness. The heavy hand
of Henry Plummer lay on the town all during 1863; at
one point Plummer even succeeded in getting elected

Virginia City's sheriff, so that he was in charge of the law in both towns at once. Plummer's chief lieutenant in Virginia City was the terrifying Boone Helm, who came roistering out of the Idaho gold camps early in 1863.

Helm and five companions started east from Idaho in mid-winter, but only Helm completed the trip alive. During his journey he teamed up for a while with a half-starved Indian and thoughtfully offered the man some meat. When the Indian asked Helm what they were eating, Helm unpacked his knapsack and held up a human leg! In Virginia City, this nightmarish character made a habit of getting drunk and sauntering down the street, a gun at each hip, ready to blaze away at anyone who looked at him the wrong way. People would scatter and take cover when they heard that Boone Helm was on the warpath. He joined the Plummer gang, and was among those hanged in January of 1864 when Plummer's crimes were exposed. Helm and four other bandits went to the gallows on January 14, 1864, four days after Plummer. During his last moments Helm noisily protested that he was an innocent man, and called for a Bible on which to swear. The infuriated vigilantes strung him up. He died a troublemaker to the end, shouting, "Hooray for Jefferson Davis!"

An even more villainous Virginia City outlaw was the notorious Jack Slade, made famous by Mark Twain's *Roughing It*. Slade was born in Illinois; when he was about twenty-six he killed a man in a quarrel and fled to the West. Mark Twain relates that

> At St. Joseph, Missouri, he joined one of the early California-bound emigrant trains, and was given the post of train-master. One day on the plains he had an angry dispute with one of his wagon-drivers, and both drew their revolvers. But the driver was the quicker artist, and had his weapon cocked first. So Slade said it was a pity to waste life on so small a matter, and proposed that the pistols be thrown on the ground and the quarrel settled by a fist-fight. The unsuspecting driver agreed, and threw down his pistol—whereupon Slade laughed at his simplicity, and shot him dead!

In the lawless West, Slade's ferocity and ruthlessness made him so well known that the Overland Stage Line offered him a job. The stagecoach company was having problems at its station at Julesburg, Colorado. Julesburg had been named for the station-keeper, a fiery French-Canadian called Jules Reni, who was suspected of stealing company horses and tipping local outlaws off to gold shipments. Jules was discharged and Slade took his place as station-keeper. As Mark Twain describes it,

> The outlaws soon found that the new agent was a man who did not fear anything that breathed the breath of life. The result was that delays ceased, the company's property was let alone, and no matter what happened or who suffered, Slade's coaches went through, every time! True, in order to bring about this wholesome change,

Slade had to kill several men—some say three, others say four, and others six—but the world was the richer for their loss.

Slade's worst trouble was with the ousted Jules, who had run Julesburg as his own private kingdom, and bitterly hated the man who had displaced him. Their rivalry grew heated after Slade hired a man Jules had once fired, and seized a team of horses that he claimed Jules had stolen from the company. For a day or two both men roamed the streets of the little town, armed and ready for a fight. As Slade stepped into a store, Jules emptied a double-barreled shotgun into his back. Slade returned the fire. Mark Twain writes,

> Then both men fell, and were carried to their respective lodgings, both swearing that better aim should do deadlier work next time. Both were bedridden a long time, but Jules got on his feet first, and gathering his possessions together, packed them on a couple of mules, and fled to the Rocky Mountains to gather strength in safety against the day of reckoning.

The Overland Stage Line, pleased with Slade's job of restoring order in Julesburg, transferred him to another station which was, according to Mark Twain, "the very paradise of outlaws and desperados. There was absolutely no semblance of law there. Violence was the rule. Force was the only recognized authority." The first time one such outlaw menaced him, Slade shot him dead. He put a stop to the raids on the stagecoach line, killed several of the most dangerous bandits, and made himself "supreme judge in his district, and jury and executioner likewise," hanging with his own hands two men who had robbed the company. Slade was totally merciless, but he kept the stagecoaches running on schedule. Thomas J. Dimsdale's *The Vigilantes of Montana*, a book published in Virginia City in 1866, declared that "Stories of Slade's hanging men, and of innumerable assaults, shootings, stabbings and beatings, in which he was a principal actor, form part of the legends of the stage line. As for minor quarrels and shootings, it is absolutely certain that a minute history of Slade's life would be one long record of such practices."

In time Slade's old enemy, Jules Reni, was captured in his mountain hideout. Mark Twain describes how

> they brought him to Rocky Ridge, bound hand and foot, and deposited him in the middle of the cattle-yard with his back against a post. It is said that the pleasure that lit Slade's face when he heard of it was something fearful to contemplate. He examined his enemy to see that he was securely tied, and then went to bed, content to wait till morning before enjoying the luxury of killing him. Jules spent the night in the cattle-yard . . . . In the morning Slade practised on him with his revolver, nipping the flesh here and there, and occasionally clipping off a finger, while Jules begged him to kill him outright and put him out of his misery. Finally Slade reloaded, and walking up to his victim, made some characteristic remarks and then dispatched him. The body

lay there half a day, nobody venturing to touch it without orders, and then Slade detailed a party and assisted
at the burial himself. But he first cut off the dead man's
ears and put them in his vest pocket, where he carried
them for some time with great satisfaction.

Mark Twain claimed to have met Slade once in the
course of his western travels. At an unnamed stagecoach
station, said the author, he

sat down to breakfast with a half-savage, half-civilized company of armed and bearded mountaineers, ranch-men, and station employees. The most gentlemanly-ap-pearing, quiet and affable officer we had yet found along the road in the Overland Company's service was the person who sat at the head of the table, at my elbow. Never youth stared and shivered as I did when I heard them call him SLADE! . . . here, right by my side, was the actual ogre who, in fights and brawls and various ways, *had taken the lives of twenty-six human beings* . . . . He was so friendly and so gentle-spoken that I warmed to him in spite of his awful history. It was hardly possible to realize that this pleasant person was the pitiless scourge of the outlaws . . . . And to this day I can remember nothing remarkable about Slade except that his face was rather broad across the cheek bones, and that the cheek bones were low and the lips pecu-liarly thin and straight.

Like any good storyteller, Mark Twain was fond of embellishing his stories a bit, and quite probably his path never did cross Slade's. But Thomas J. Dimsdale of Virginia City undoubtedly did see the famed murderer in action, and commented, "Those who saw him in his natural state only, would pronounce him to be a kind husband, a most hospitable host and a courteous gentle-man; on the contrary, those who met him when mad-dened with liquor and surrounded by a gang of armed roughs, would pronounce him a fiend incarnate."

Slade's reign of terror at the Rocky Mountains stage-coach station began to bring the company some bad publicity, and he lost his job. In the spring of 1863 he arrived in Virginia City, which had just been founded. In a town of tough men, Slade was the toughest. He was drinking heavily now, and, Dimsdale's *Vigilantes of Montana* says,

> He . . . might often be seen galloping through the streets, shouting and yelling, firing revolvers, etc. On many occasions he would ride his horse into stores, break up bars, toss the scales out of doors and use most insulting language to parties present . . . . It had become quite common, when Slade was on a spree, for the shopkeepers and citizens to close the stores and put out all the lights; being fearful of some outrage at his hands. For his wanton destruction of goods and furniture, he was always ready to pay, when sober, if he had money; but there were not a few who regarded payments as small satisfaction for the outrage, and these men were his personal enemies.

Slade never killed anyone in Virginia City. In fact, when he was sober he operated on the side of the law. He took part in the vigilante activities that rounded up the Plummer gang, and was responsible for bringing several criminals to justice. Everyone in town knew of his reputation as a killer, of course, but he claimed that all of his past crimes had been committed for the sake of keeping order.

After the hanging of Plummer's five lieutenants on January 14, 1864, Virginia City felt a great yearning for tranquility. A permanent court system was established so that outlaws could be tried by judge and jury. Slade was one of the first victims of this reform. He had gathered about himself an assortment of followers and and admirers drawn from the worst elements in town. Many of the more sober citizens feared that these armed ruffians would eventually take the place of the defeated Plummer mob and create chaos in Montana. One night Slade and his friends got violently drunk and shot up the town. Although he still had committed no crime more serious than disorderly conduct, the time had come to bring him under control. In the morning, Sheriff J. M. Fox confronted Slade amid a group of his cohorts and presented a warrant for his arrest. Dimsdale says that Slade "became uncontrollably furious, and seizing the writ, he tore it up, threw it on the ground and stamped upon it. The clicking of the locks of his companions' revolvers was instantly heard, and a crisis was expected."

The sheriff, a cautious man as well as a brave one, did not attempt to arrest Slade, but let him withdraw, "leaving Slade the master of the situation and the conqueror and ruler of the courts, law and lawmakers. This was a declaration of war, and was so accepted. The Vigilance Committee now felt that the question of social order and the preponderance of the law-abiding citizens had then and there to be decided. They knew the character of Slade, and they were well aware that they must

submit to his rule without murmur, or else that he must
be dealt with. . . ."

A leading vigilante who happened also to be one of
Slade's friends warned him to get out of town for his
own good before a showdown arrived. Instead Slade,
who was still drunk, sought out Alexander Davis, the
judge of Virginia City's new court, put a gun to his
head, and told him that he was being held as a hostage
for Slade's safety. The judge remained calm. News of
this outrage spread through Alder Gulch, and the miners
of Nevada City decided that the time had come to get
rid of Slade. Some six hundred of them marched up to
Virginia City to meet with the local vigilantes. In Virginia City there was still a great deal of hesitance about
hanging Slade, annoying and potentially dangerous
though he was; but the hot-tempered miners prevailed.
A search party went in quest of Slade.

When he learned what was happening, Slade sobered
instantly and even apologized to Judge Davis. But it was
too late. The vigilantes surrounded him, informed him
that his doom had come, and asked him if he had any
business that required settling. Without much delay
they rigged a gallows on the gateposts of a corral. The
rope was strung from a sturdy beam across the top of
the gate, and a drygoods box served as a platform. "To
this place Slade was marched," wrote Dimsdale, "surrounded by a guard, composing the best armed and most

numerous force that has ever appeared in Montana Territory."

Meanwhile a messenger had gone off to notify Slade's wife, who lived with him on a ranch outside town. Dimsdale relates how "In an instant she was in the saddle, and with all the energy that love and despair could lend to an ardent temperament and a strong physique, she urged her fleet charger over the twelve miles of rough and rocky ground that intervened between her and the object of her passionate devotion."

Slade seemed astonished that Virginia City meant to hang him. He poured forth tears, prayers, and lamentations, exclaiming again and again, "My God! my God! must I die? Oh, my dear wife!" The posse members nodded sympathetically, for they admired Slade's courage and his marksmanship, and deeply regretted that his bloodthirsty, reckless ways, and his open defiance of the court left them no choice but to execute him. Many of the onlookers wept. Slade begged to be allowed to see his wife before he was hanged; but the vigilantes feared that she might interfere with the proceedings if they waited any longer, and that she might lead an uprising of Slade's followers. Dimsdale writes:

"Everything being ready, the command was given, 'Men, do your duty,' and the box being instantly slipped from beneath his feet, he died almost instantaneously.

"The body was cut down and carried to the Virginia

Hotel, where in a darkened room, it was scarcely laid out, when the unfortunate and bereaved companion of the deceased arrived, at headlong speed, to find that all was over, and that she was a widow. Her grief and heart-piercing cries were terrible evidences of the depth of her attachment for her lost husband." One story has it that she brought Slade's corpse home and sealed it in a metal coffin filled with alcohol. When she left soon after for Salt Lake City, she took the sloshing coffin with her.

Alder Gulch yielded over $120,000,000 in gold, but nearly all of this tremendous bonanza was taken out in the wild early years when Henry Plummer and Jack Slade were riding high. The land around Virginia City was so rich in those years that almost anyone might find gold anywhere. One of Virginia City's more picturesque characters, a certain Bummer Dan, found it easier to beg and steal from the miners than to do any work himself, and this so irritated the hard-working citizens that they gave him a pick and a shovel, marched him to a worth-less-looking claim high above the gulch, and told him to get busy—or else. Gloomily he began to dig, pausing frequently to rest. The miners left him there, and when they came back later to check on his progress they found him feverishly cutting through pay dirt. He had found one of the richest mines thereabouts. Quickly he col-lected a few thousand dollars' worth of gold, packed up, and announced that he was heading East. Road agents intercepted the stage coach and parted him from his gold, and in a little while he was back in Virginia City, a panhandler once more.

The easy money was gone by 1870, and Virginia City's population dropped from something over 10,000 to just 2,555. More than half of those were gone by 1880, although some mining continued. An article published in 1879 said, "Now that she has become a steady business city she is not compelled to depend on the former placers, but looks with pride at the strides made in the agricultural valleys that contribute the elements of life and prosperity." The combination of agriculture and steady, small-scale mining kept Virginia City alive in a sleepy way while other boom towns of Montana were going under. The population dipped to six hundred by the turn of the century, and by easy stages sank below four hundred. Gold still came in modest quantities from the quartz veins of Alder Gulch, though, and the mines have never altogether closed.

Virginia City today is one of those not-quite ghost towns, reconstructed for the delight of tourists, which create the illusion of an authentic city of the old West. Much of the town came down to our time in good condition, and a good deal has been restored by Montanans. Among the highlights are Rank's Drug Store, which has been in continuous operation since 1864, and the Bale of Hay Saloon, where antique nickelodeons and music boxes tinkle away with the melodies of yesteryear.

A museum displays relics of the gold-rush days; the Variety Theatre runs an annual summer festival of melodramas in which college students perform creaky old thrillers while the audience hisses the villain and cheers the hero. Wooden sidewalks, the soft glow of gas lights, dozens of stores stocked with merchandise of the last century, all help to create the remarkable illusion of a trip backward in time. And—so they say—the ghosts of Henry Plummer, Jack Slade, and the other legendary bad men of Montana's early days still flit about, scowling at strangers, lurking in dark alleys, and plotting dire revenge on the forces of law and order.

TEN
Ghost Towns
of the Southwest

THE PROSPECTORS WHO STAMPEDED first to California, then to Nevada, Colorado, Utah, Idaho, and Montana paid little heed to the cactus country of Arizona and New Mexico. The southwestern territories were virtually the last parts of the West to be exploited for their mineral wealth in the nineteenth century, although Spaniards had begun the quest for North American gold there four hundred years earlier. Coronado, searching for the mythical Seven Cities of Cíbola in 1540, had explored New Mexico without luck, but other Spaniards later in the century had found silver mines in the hills. Little came of these early discoveries. Early in the nineteenth century, Mexican settlers in the area had opened gold and copper mines, and placer miners were at work long before Jim Marshall's California find. In 1846 an American army officer at San Pedro, northeast of Albuquerque, New Mexico, described these activities in a report to Congress:

> In the evening we visited a town at the base of the principal mountain; here, mingled with houses, were huge mounds of earth, thrown out of the wells so that the village looked like a village of gigantic prairie-dogs. Nearly all the people there were at their wells, and were drawing up bags of loose sand by means of windlasses. Around little pools, men, women, and children were grouped, intently poring over these bags of loose sand, washing the earth in wooden platters or goat horns.

Yet it was a long time before anyone did any serious mining there. In 1880 a town site was laid out and the San Pedro Milling Company constructed reservoirs in adjoining canyons, bringing water by pipes to the placer deposits. Both gold and copper mining was carried on until a prolonged drought shut down operations in 1883. Four years later, the discovery of a rich gold mine got things going again, and when a big copper deposit came to light San Pedro enjoyed a brief but giddy boom. A newspaper, the *Golden 9*, published its first issue on July 18, 1889; how long it lasted is unknown, for only that issue and a second one still exist. The first number declared:

> People from afar contemplating removing to San Pedro will do well to ponder on a few hints we have compiled for their benefit. Bring a tent. If this is not

possible, then bring along wagon sheets, canvas, table covers, door mats, gunny sacks, umbrellas, etc. with which to improvise a tent-shack or tepee in which to live until you can make a dug-out or build a house . . . . There are no vacant houses in town . . . . There are families here living in coke ovens. Others have nothing but a town lot.

The newspaper told of the luck of one Mr. Kelly, who stopped into the office to display "a little gold button which only weighed 23 ounces and was worth only $425." Another man bought a lot for a house, washed out some $1,000 in placer gold in his back yard, and struck an underground vein of gold. "Everybody is coming to San Pedro," the paper declared. But the gold fizzled out and the copper mine, after yielding several million pounds between 1889 and 1892, also ran bare. San Pedro became a ghost town of ruined shacks and decaying adobe huts, although from time to time copper shortages have caused its mines to be re-explored.

In the same part of the state is the town of Cerrillos, one of New Mexico's oldest settlements. The Indians had mined silver and the semiprecious stone turquoise here for hundreds of years when the Spaniards first arrived. Using Indian slave labor, the Spaniards continued to mine the low, rounded hills (*cerrillos* in Spanish) and named their town for them. Gold was discovered in 1722 and again in 1823, but the policies of the Spanish and Mexican government officials kept all strangers out and prevented gold rushes from developing.

In 1879, more than thirty years after the United States had seized possession of New Mexico in the Mexican War, American prospectors rediscovered the Cerrillos mines. They found Indian stone axes in the old shafts—along with enough silver, gold, and turquoise to start a boom. A cluster of mining camps sprang up around Cerrillos. The Atchison, Topeka & Santa Fe Railroad ran its tracks there from Santa Fe. Cerrillos grew to a population of 2,500 that enjoyed the services of twenty-one saloons.

When the gold and silver petered out, the camps around Cerrillos became ghost towns, but Cerrillos survived because it had struck a humbler but quite useful mineral: coal. Coal from Cerrillos powered the smoke-belching locomotives of the Santa Fe Railroad for many years. After World War II, though, the railroad converted to diesel fuel and Cerrillos, lacking a market for its coal, faced extinction. The town converted itself into a tourist center, however, and probably is here to stay. The heart of activities is the Tiffany Saloon in the middle of town—founded in the 1860's and originally owned by the Tiffany jewelry family of New York, which then operated a turquoise mine near Cerrillos. From April to November the saloon offers food and liquid refreshments in the style of the old West. Many of its furnishings are authentically old, including the twenty-two-foot walnut bar with brass footrail.

Back of the saloon is a theater where college students present old-time melodramas in the summer, a standard feature of many revived ghost towns. Down the street is the splendid Palace Hotel, a stone and adobe building erected in 1880. A museum and curio shop has exhibits and items for sale, as well as the town's lone public telephone, and sells soft drinks. There is even some mining around Cerrillos again. About 1900, Thomas A. Edison tried to collect the very fine gold dust of the region with static electricity. It did not work, but today weekend miners pan for gold dust using a "dry" placer machine that separates gold from dirt with blasts of air. The yield is said to be on the meager side.

In the mountains northeast of Santa Fe is Elizabethtown, the home of 7,000 people in 1868, a ghost town today. Its last moments of glory came about 1901, when a big gold dredge went to work cleaning up the pay dirt that the early placer miners had left behind. Eventually the dredging stopped and the dredge itself sank into the sand of the stream bed until it disappeared. A visitor in 1951 found "E-town" deserted:

> The wind blew in cutting blasts across its treeless streets. On the crown of one low hill is a church, built of stained and weathered boards; on the top of another hill is the cemetery. Below the church, which dominates the townsite, stands a schoolhouse, and in front of that are two or three terraced, grass-grown streets, reached by rutted roads. Tall sagebrush hides many of the foundation holes, in which debris and fragments of sun-tinted lavender glass lie jumbled together. In one the carcass of an upright piano lies flat upon its back.

Dozens of such forlorn ghost towns dot the deserts of New Mexico. The cycle of boom and bust has been particularly harsh there. Neighboring Arizona, too, is well supplied with such relics of bygone excitement. Exaggerated reports of Mexican luck in Arizona's silver mines helped to encourage the arrival of prospectors after Arizona passed into the possession of the United States, but a mining boom in the 1850's ran out of steam quickly. Placer gold discovered on the banks of the Gila River near its meeting with the Colorado River in 1858 started a second equally brief stampede. One town that was born then was Gila City, which had 1,200 miners at one time. When the placer deposits gave out in 1864, the prospectors moved a short way up the Colorado to the town of La Paz, where new "color" had been sighted two years before.

La Paz had a breathless seven-year boom in which $8,000,000 in gold dust and nuggets came from the river bed. It prospered for another reason: there was still no rail transportation in this part of the country, and La Paz became an important river port. Clipper ships and steamers brought cargo to the mouth of the Colorado River in the Gulf of California, and there it was loaded upon light steamers that carried it inland along the navigable stretches of the Colorado. Goods and produce traveled upstream, while the gold and silver from the mining camps was shipped downstream, and La Paz was one of the chief harbors of this trade.

Then double catastrophe struck in 1870. The turbulent Colorado River changed its course, leaving La Paz a mile from water and ruining it as a port. About the same time the placer deposits gave out, and La Paz joined the ranks of the ghost towns.

There were scattered gold and silver strikes in Arizona during the 1860's and 1870's, but the territory aroused little enthusiasm among prospectors until Ed Schieffelin brought in the Lucky Cuss silver mine in 1878. This started the boom that created Tombstone, probably the most famous and least ghostly of all the ghost towns of the old West.

Schieffelin was no old forty-niner. He belonged to the younger generation of prospectors, for he was born in Pennsylvania in 1848, some months after Jim Marshall's great find at Sutter's Mill. When he was ten years old Schieffelin was taken to California, and by the time he was seventeen he was working a claim in Oregon. He tried his luck in Nevada, Utah, and Idaho as much for the fun of it as for the hope of striking it rich. By January 1877, he was ready to see what Arizona might hold.

With two mules and a pack outfit he entered the territory, going down into the parched country south of Tucson near the Mexican border. That was no place for casual visitors in 1877. The Apache Indians were on the warpath, and United States troops, stationed at Fort Huachuca, were trying to put them down. Schieffelin got a cool welcome when he showed up at the fort in April and announced that he proposed to hunt for mines. "Someday you'll find your tombstone," the soldiers warned him, and tried to get him to keep out of the dangerous country.

Schieffelin ignored their grim predictions. He rode out each day with the troops, sniffing around in the desert and counting on them for protection. When he grew more familiar with the region he started going out alone, spending all day prospecting and returning to the fort at night. Gradually he roamed farther and farther from the fort, into the hills to the east. He set up camp on the highest hill in the vicinity, where it was impossible for anyone to sneak up unseen on him, and in August 1877, he found an outcropping of silver ore. He staked a claim and named it the Tombstone as a somber jest. When he found a second ore deposit nearby, he called the claim the Graveyard.

Schieffelin took his rock samples to Tucson, hoping to raise money for a mining operation, but no one seemed interested in them. In October he returned to his two claims, gathered a bag of ore, and headed for Silver King, well to the north, where a medium-big mining camp had sprouted in 1876. Schieffelin's brother Al had been working there; but by the time he arrived at Silver King, his brother had moved along to an even more distant camp. Finally Schieffelin caught up with him and proudly displayed his samples, only to have Al shrug and dismiss them as worthless.

An assayer and mining engineer named Richard Gird took a close look at Schieffelin's ore, though, and decided to go to the trouble of running an assay. He performed tests that showed that the ore from the Tombstone claim amounted to very little, but the Graveyard samples proved out at $2,000 a ton. That was respectable enough. Gird proposed to finance an expedition to the Schieffelin claims; in return for his money he would share equally in the finds with the two brothers.

In February of 1878 the three men visited the sites where Ed Schieffelin had done his prospecting. At first it seemed that they had been too optimistic; the Tombstone and Graveyard claims turned out to contain nothing but small pockets of ore surrounded by worthless rock. But they kept looking, reasoning that there had to be a vein of silver somewhere nearby, and shortly they came upon a major lode assaying $15,000 a ton. They named it the Lucky Cuss. Soon afterward they located the Tough Nut mine.

Prospectors arrived by the dozens, seemingly springing up out of the sands of the desert. Two of them, Hank Williams and John Oliver, discovered another silver mine and got into a long, bitter dispute with Dick Gird about its ownership. After much discussion the mine was divided. Gird and the Schieffelin brothers named their section the Contention; Oliver and Williams called theirs the Grand Central. These two mines plus the Lucky Cuss and Tough Nut were destined to be the cornerstone of the district's wealth. The Contention alone produced $1,676,000 in 1882, and in the first five years of operations its yield was better than $5,000,000. It did not pour all this money into the pockets of Gird and the Schieffelins, though, for they sold their rights in the mine for $10,000 in the spring of 1878. (Luckily for them, they held onto the Lucky Cuss and the Tough Nut a little longer.)

In the summer of 1878 it became clear that a major bonanza was at hand, and outside investors started to move in. A. P. K. Safford, the governor of Arizona Territory, offered to put up the money for further development and exploitation of the Schieffelin-Gird properties, in return for a quarter interest. The four partners formed the Tombstone Mining and Milling Company. The mining camp of Tombstone began to take form.

In 1879 Gird supervised the construction of the mining company's mill. Since there was no satisfactory water supply for mill operations at Tombstone, Gird had to go nine miles away, to the banks of the San Pedro River. Here the town of Millville, later called Charleston, was founded. Five huge mills were built to pound the Tombstone ore. Gird also put up the Big House, a massive adobe office building with walls three feet thick. Its chief feature was a giant steel safe in which silver bullion supposedly was stored while awaiting shipment to San Francisco. The safe was only a decoy designed to keep any thieves who might break in from finding the silver, which was actually hidden in secret wallpaper-covered panels in the walls. The Big House was invaded by bandits only once, in 1833. They killed the bookkeeper because he was too slow in opening the safe, but they found no silver.

Charleston was an active and vigorous town in the old days—it is only a ruin today—but it was never anything more than a suburb of Tombstone. Tombstone became a city of respectable size, if not of respectable character, with a population of close to fifteen thousand. The growth was swift and spectacular. Along Allen Street, the main thoroughfare, saloons and gambling palaces kept their doors open twenty-four hours a day. The finest theater in town was Schieffelin Hall, on the corner of Fremont and Fourth streets, built by Ed Schieffelin's brother Al in 1881. It was said to have the biggest stage between Denver and San Francisco. An amateur troupe, the Tombstone Dramatic Association, gave the first performance there on September 15, 1881: *The Ticket-of-Leave Man*. Three months later a professional group, the Nellie Boyd Dramatic Company, delighted the miners with *The Banker's Daughter*. By the following year Tombstone was important enough to play host to nearly every troupe of traveling actors touring the West. For more intimate entertainment there were the variety theaters, such as the Bird Cage, which opened in 1881 on the day after Christmas. Masquerades, balls, and lively vaudeville shows were held on its tiny stage, while waitresses circulated through the hall to sell drinks to the patrons, singing as they worked.

Tombstone prided itself on its toughness. It had more

than its share of rough customers, and many of them found early graves in Tombstone's Boothill Cemetery. The weatherbeaten markers in the cemetery tell grim stories of violence:

Here lies Lester Moore
Four slugs from a .44
No less, no more

          *   *   *

Harry Curry—'82
Killed by Indians

          *   *   *

Red River Tom—Shot by Ormsby

          *   *   *

Bronco Charlie—Shot by Ormsby

          *   *   *

Ormsby—Shot

          *   *   *

One set of markers records the resting places of Tom McLowery, his brother Frank, and Billy Clanton—the victims in the most famous event in Tombstone's history, the gunfight at the O. K. Corral. This epic battle grew out of a feud between two sets of brothers, one on the side of the law and one outside it. The outlaws were Ike and Billy Clanton; the lawmen were Virgil Earp, the city marshal of Tombstone, and his brothers

Morgan and Wyatt. On October 27, 1881, the Clanton boys came swaggering into town, armed and full of liquor, bragging that they were going to "get" the Earps. Accompanying the Clantons were the Mc-Lowery brothers and Billy Claiborne, three tough cowboys who also disliked the Earps.

The Earp brothers heard that the outlaws had gathered in the O. K. Corral on Fremont Street. At half-past two the Earps started toward the corral, accompanied by Doc Holliday, a gunslinging dentist from Georgia. That evening's edition of Tombstone's newspaper tells what happened:

> The marshall [Virgil Earp] called out, "Boys, throw up your hands; I want you to give up your shooters."
> At this Frank McLowery attempted to draw his pistol when Wyatt Earp immediately shot him, the ball entering just above the waist. Doc Holliday then let go at Tom McLowery with a shotgun, filling him full of buckshot under the right arm. Billy Clanton then blazed away at Marshall Earp, and Ike Clanton, who it is claimed was unarmed started and ran off through the corral to Allen street. The firing then became general, and some thirty shots were fired, all in such rapid succession that the fight was over in less than a minute.
> When the smoke cleared away it was found that Frank McLowery had been killed outright . . . . Tom McLowery lay dead around the corner on Third street . . . . Billy Clanton lay on the side of the street, with one shot in the right waist and another in the right side

near the wrist, and the third in the left breast. He was taken into a house and lived half an hour in great agony.

Morgan Earp was shot through both shoulders, the ball creasing the skin. Marshall Earp was shot through the fleshy part of the right leg. Wyatt Earp and Doc Holliday escaped unhurt.

The shooting created great excitement and the street

was immediately filled with people. Ike Clanton was captured and taken to jail . . . . The feeling of the better class of citizens is that the marshall and his posse acted solely in the right in attempting to disarm the cowboys and that it was a case of kill or be killed.

The rights and wrongs of the gunfight at the O. K. Corral have been debated ever since, and the argument still rages among the latter-day residents of Tombstone. Some say that the Earps and Doc Holliday murdered the McLowerys and Billy Clanton in cold blood as the climax to their long feud. Others claim that the killings were justified in the name of the law. The gunfight is re-enacted at Tombstone every October for the benefit of visitors who want to draw their own conclusions.

Billy Claiborne, who survived the slaughter at the corral, gained his plot in Boothill Cemetery not much later. He made the mistake of picking a drunken quarrel with Buckskin Frank Leslie, the bartender at the Oriental Saloon. Leslie told Claiborne to take his business elsewhere. Angry at being ejected, the cowboy went to get a shotgun to teach Buckskin Frank a lesson. A friend warned Leslie that Claiborne was returning. He set his cigar down on the Oriental's polished bar, drew his .45, and slipped out of the tavern through a side door. Going around to the front where Claiborne awaited him, Leslie took aim and quietly called, "Billy." Claiborne turned and got a bullet through the heart. Buckskin Frank coolly went back inside, picked up his cigar, and commented to a waiting customer, "He died nice."

Another set of Boothill grave markers commemorates some bloody doings of 1884. A gang of six outlaws had gone on a spree in the nearby town of Bisbee, robbing the payroll of a mining company and shooting up the town, killing a number of people. They were captured and brought to Tombstone for trial. Bob Heath, the leader of the gang, was tried first. The jury convicted him of nothing more serious than second-degree murder—a verdict that called only for imprisonment, not for hanging. This decision did not sit well with the local citizens, who hauled Heath from jail and strung him up. His gravestone reads:

Taken from County Jail and lynched
by Bisbee mob in Tombstone, Feb. 22, 1884

The jurors were warned that they had best not be so generous to the other five murderers. In due course they were all found guilty of first-degree murder and sentenced to be hanged. Never before had Tombstone had a legal execution, although there had been plenty of lynchings. The occasion was a formal one: the sheriff issued special invitations marked "Not Transferable!" which entitled selected guests to witness the executions, beginning at 1:00 P.M at the Tombstone courthouse. The hangman had a busy afternoon, and the wooden grave marker declares:

Dan Dowd
Red Sample
Tex Howard
Bill DeLaney
Dan Kelly
LEGALLY
Hanged
Mar 8 1884.

Not all the graves in Boothill are those of men who died by violence. One marker reads:

John Blair died of Smallpox
Cowboy threw rope over feet
and dragged him to his grave

Another marks the resting place of one of Tombstone's oldest inhabitants, a Negro who had been a slave belonging to Sheriff John Slaughter:

JOHN SWAIN (SLAUGHTER)
Born June 1846. Former Slave who came to
Tombstone 1879. Died February 8, 1946.
Erected by the Personnel at Fort Huachuca
and Friends of Tombstone in Memory of a
Worthy Pioneer.

Sheriff Slaughter himself, who kept the law in Tombstone for four difficult years in the 1880's, is buried elsewhere; he died peacefully in California. Doc Holliday, the sharpshooting dentist, is interred in Colorado, where he died of tuberculosis. "I had offered odds of eight to five," he said, "that I'd cash out some day at the end of a six-shooter. Tough to lose that bet." He died in bed with his boots off, against the odds. His last words were, "This is funny."

Ed Schieffelin, who sold out his share of the silver mines in 1880 for a medium-big fortune and moved to Los Angeles, did not want to be buried in Boothill. He lies on the hill overlooking Tombstone where he first struck silver ore, with his pick and shovel and canteen at his side in the grave.

Most of the inhabitants of Boothill were put to rest there before 1900, but some, like the ex-slave John Swain, received burial fairly recently. Quong Kee, Tombstone's last Chinese pioneer, was buried there in 1938. Born in Hong Kong, or perhaps Canton, Quong Kee left China about 1863 and settled as a cook's helper in Virginia City, Montana, where he watched the downfall of the Plummer gang. "All the time in Virginia City someone get robbed," he said many years later. "Bang, someone die in the streets. When the vigilantes come, they brave men. They catch robbers and hang five in one day. Plenty excitement in Virginia City." When the Montana boom ended, Quong Kee cooked for the men who were building the first transcontinental railroad, the Union Pacific. The railroad was finished in

1869, and he settled in Stockton, California, running a restaurant whose profits were high enough to let him make a sentimental journey back to China.

Upon his return from China he heard of the silver strikes in Arizona and moved to Tombstone. He and his cousin Ah Lum opened the Can Can Restaurant, where the Earp brothers often ate, as did their enemies the Clanton brothers. Of Billy Clanton, killed at the O. K. Corral, Quong Kee said, "He good man, always paid his bills." The old Chinese restaurateur stayed on in Tombstone long after the town's fortunes had waned. He closed the Can Can and had to live on charity, and when he died he was buried in a pauper's unmarked grave in the town of Bisbee. The few remaining citizens of Tombstone heard of this and raised a fund to give him a proper funeral in the town where he had lived so long, and all of Arizona sent delegations for such an unusual event as a burial in Boothill Cemetery.

The last burial of all at Boothill took place in 1953. Glenn Will, who won fame under the nickname of Bronco Bill, left instructions when he died that he was to be buried at Tombstone. The old man was cremated and his ashes were shipped there—C.O.D. The Chamber of Commerce paid the delivery charges of $1.92 and found a place for Bronco Bill.

All these events—from the gunfight at the O. K. Corral to the burial of Bronco Bill seventy-two years later —were recorded in Tombstone's newspaper, the *Epi-*

taph. The name was a logical one. "What is Tombstone without an Epitaph?" asked a newspaperman when the town was just getting started, and the paper, one of the liveliest in the West, was founded. The pages of the *Epitaph* tell of Tombstone's rise and fall and of its modern resurrection.

One of the favorite sports of Tombstone in the old days was claim-jumping. As in any mining camp, the discoverer of a likely-looking ore deposit could claim the right to mine it simply by filing the proper form at the nearest courthouse. But if he failed to start work at the site within a certain length of time, anyone else could "re-locate" or claim the site anew. An article in the *Epitaph* for August 6, 1887, described some of the refinements of this practice:

> If a miner has not complied with all the requirements of law, his claim (or mine) can, on the second New Year's day following the date of location, be re-located by himself or others, who may be on the ground before him . . . . A person stuck up notices on a claim near a cabin in which three men were sleeping, awaiting early morning to locate it. The locater, after securing the claim, thoughtfully woke the boys to tell them they needn't get up so early, as the claim was located.
>
> One party on a location, who owned it until 12 o'clock, stood two others off until that hour on his rights as owner. At exactly 12, he put his notice in the split-stakes, and sang 12 o'clock before the others, who had no watch, knew what time it was, and then drove off.

A prospector started out with his notice written and in his pocket. He lost it on the way, seven miles from town, had no pencil or paper, and returned home, while another man located the claim.

There was a little episode in Quigley's Gulch, wherein three bad partners had made it up to relocate themselves in a claim and leave out the fourth partner. The latter had previously been warned against coming upon the claim that night, and was told by a friend that his partners were going to relocate it all to themselves; so he secured a rifle, and after the three bad partners had gone up to the mine, he crawled up on the shady side of the gulch to a cabin below the claim about 100 yards and there watched. At 11:45 his partners started up to stake the ground, whereupon, with a fearful yell, he turned loose with his gun, and could see the crusted snow fly, at every pop just over his partners' heads. They heard the bullets humming so near their ears that a panic seized them and they fled for town. As soon as they were out of sight he quietly walked up and located it all to himself, and left his bad partners out in the cold.

A well-known Bullion* miner named Mike Hynes had told all the town he had several rich locations to jump between the noted mines. Before Christmas day he had a draughtsman and expert to draw off his notices and put each one in a box on the claims he intended jumping. Being a little behind time on New Year's Eve, he was coming up the gulch to tack up his boxes, and the first square view he got of his intended claims was one calculated to make his hair stand on end as sitting on each of the seven claims and upon each of the seven

* Bullion was a camp near Tombstone.

boxes was a man, and each man had a Winchester re-
peating rifle pointed at Mike, who was so amazed that
he passed by each one! merely remarking "Good evening, Happy New Year!" And he didn't feel very well
until he got to a saloon at Bullion, where he braced up
and remarked that he guessed he hadn't lost any mines,
and he wouldn't give $5 for all he had come to jump.

Tombstone's best years were the early 1880's. The
mine shafts got deeper and deeper; but when they
reached the 500-foot level they hit the water table, or
underground water supply, and the tunnels began to
flood. The Grand Central and Contention mining companies installed huge pumps to keep the shafts dry. The
Grand Central's pump, which cost $300,000, was put
out of commission by a fire in 1885. A year later, fire
destroyed the pumping works and the hoist of the Contention. Both mines had to close. Since the giant pumps
had also been draining the smaller adjoining mines, they
too started to fill with water, so that by 1890 nearly all
mining activities in and around Tombstone were forced
to cease.

No one mining company could afford to restore the
pumps, but all the companies under one management
would be able to put up the necessary capital. In 1901
the Tombstone Consolidated Mining Company went
into business, comprising all of the older companies
rolled into one giant corporation. The new company
dug a shaft more than 1,000 feet deep and put in pumps

capable of taking out 8,000,000 gallons of water a day. Tombstone's population, which had dropped below 2,000 during the years that the mines were closed, began to increase again. But the cost of running the pumps was immense—fuel oil alone came to $700 a day—and the mines no longer were rich enough to support such expenses. When the pumps were damaged by carelessness in 1909, the cost of repairing them proved a fatal burden for the Tombstone Consolidated Mining Company. Mining and pumping operations ended altogether in January 1911, and the following August the company was declared bankrupt. Mining at Tombstone never recovered.

Oblivion threatened the desert town. The historic buildings were gnawed by decay. Weeds and debris covered Boothill Cemetery, which was used as a town garbage dump by the few remaining residents. The massive courthouse and the monumental town hall were empty and silent. Of the original fifteen city blocks, only two or three remained.

In 1925 history-conscious Arizonans began to salvage what was left of Tombstone. They removed the debris, restored a few of the old buildings, touched up the markers in the cemetery, and, using the slogan, "The Town Too Tough to Die," began transforming Tombstone into a tourist center. The *Epitaph* continued to appear on a weekly basis. A few of the theaters of the 1880's presented contemporary shows. The revival of

Tombstone gained momentum in 1964, when a lawyer from Detroit visited the town, became fascinated with it, and organized a company to buy up the original sections and keep them in good repair. In the first two years of the project more than $2,000,000 was spent. The easterners paid $30,000 for Schieffelin Hall and laid out $100,000 more to restore it. The cost of purchasing the Crystal Palace Saloon and transforming it into a replica of its 1881 self was $190,000; the lamps hanging from the ceiling, exact duplicates of the long-vanished originals, cost $300 apiece. They bought the O. K. Corral and put a guide on duty to show visitors the exact spots where the McLowery boys and Billy Clanton bit the dust. Among the important sites not owned by the Detroit group are the Bird Cage Theater, the Lucky Cuss Restaurant, and the Wells Fargo office, now a museum.

Tombstone today glitters with renewed splendor. For those who prefer to see what happens to a ghost town when no one cares to undo time's ravages, the surrounding desert offers grim examples in such ruined mill towns as Charleston and Contention City, only a few miles away. Their fate might have been the fate of Tombstone—except that someone cared.

An Arizona mining town of a later era, now trying to make a comeback as a tourist center after a spell of ghostliness, is Jerome, which lies between Phoenix and

Flagstaff amid some of the state's most spectacular scenery.

More than a thousand years ago, Indians were attracted to the brilliant outcroppings of minerals on the steep mountainsides there. They were too primitive to have any use for metals, but the richly colored ores were desirable for decorating pottery, clothing, and their own bodies. When the Spaniards visited the area in 1598, they found the shallow shaft that the Indians had used when mining for the green, blue, and brown pigments they prized. A Spanish explorer marked the site on a chart, but never returned to give the mine a closer look.

A scout named Al Sieber climbed the mountain about 1873 and found the mine once more. The most important metal present was copper. A few years later, some prospectors from the town of Prescott, twenty-five miles to the southwest, staked claims there but did not work them. This kind of casual prospecting went on until 1882, with no significant results.

By then two noteworthy things had happened. A railroad line had reached the vicinity, so that heavy mining equipment could be carried in for the first time; and the claims of most of the early prospectors had been bought up by Frederick A. Tritle, Arizona's newly appointed territorial governor. Governor Tritle proposed to begin large-scale copper mining on Mingus Mountain, where the richest outcroppings were located. Because he did not have enough money to finance the development work, Tritle brought in an easterner as his partner—a New York lawyer named Eugene Jerome. Jerome, whose cousin Jennie had married an English aristocrat and was the mother of a small boy named Winston Churchill, agreed to put up the necessary cash —provided the mining town was named for him.

In 1883 the town of Jerome was founded, and the United Verde Copper Company went into operation. From its Big Hole mine came not only copper but such incidentals as gold and silver. Though the mining company was successful, Jerome grew slowly; it began with a population of four hundred, with fifty houses, three stores, and six saloons, and unlike most boom camps it remained small for its first few years. When the price of copper fell in 1885 from nineteen cents a pound to eleven cents, the mine closed altogether. It passed from its original owners into the hands of the ambitious, dynamic Senator William A. Clark of Montana, who undertook a tremendous development program to make the mine profitable again.

Senator Clark put a million dollars into expanding the mine. To house his miners he built a string of wooden shacks clinging precariously to the steep sides of Mingus Mountain, and also put up the Montana House, a vast stone hotel that could hold more than one thousand people. Within a decade Jerome had a population of more than ten thousand. Three times between 1897 and 1900 the wooden buildings were laid waste by fire, and three times they were built again. Jerome learned to take a light-hearted view of these fires; an 1899 headline declared, JEROME BURNS AGAIN! ENTIRE BUSINESS DISTRICT OF 24 SALOONS AND 14 CHINESE RESTAURANTS DESTROYED.

The biggest years lay ahead. About 1910 a number of new copper mines were opened, and Jerome was flooded with prospectors and get-rich-quick stock speculators. The richest of the new mines was the Little Daisy, opened in 1916 by the United Verde Extension Company. It soon overshadowed even the fabulous Big Hole mine that had started the original excitement.

Senator Clark had a giant mill and smelter constructed in the valley below Jerome, and put in a railroad line to carry ore down the mountain from the mines. Altogether some eighty-five miles of tunnels honeycombed Mingus Mountain, and tracks a mile long ran to the mill. The smelter belched fumes day and night, transforming ore into gleaming metal at the cost of killing all the vegetation for miles around.

By the 1920's Jerome had a population of fifteen thousand, living in wooden houses propped on stilts and arranged in spiraling streets going up and up the mountain. Copper was in heavy demand and it looked as though there would be no limit to Jerome's good fortune. But in 1925 an omen of doom appeared: dynamite blasts within the mountain, intended to clear the way to new ore deposits, threatened to send the entire town tumbling into the valley. Landslides began and could not be halted. Buildings slipped downhill at a rate of several inches a year. The city jail traveled more than one hundred feet from its original place; the post office, a movie theater, and a big store dropped down the slope, and many other buildings cracked or collapsed. Timbers and steel cables were used to shore them up, and finally the worst of the landslides ceased, although some people still think that a single good sneeze would shoot the whole town into the valley.

The peak year was 1929. A year later, the nation was in the grip of a depression, and the price of copper began to skid even faster downhill than the buildings of Jerome. When it reached five cents a pound, the mining companies started to give up. The United Verde mine closed down first. In 1935 it was purchased by Phelps Dodge, a large copper company, for a mere $20,000,000 —less than the Big Hole had produced per year in its best days. In 1938 the United Verde Extension Company went out of business as the Little Daisy mine ceased to be profitable, and two years later Phelps Dodge halted work at the Big Hole, which had reached a depth of one thousand feet in its sixty-odd years of development.

During World War II the demand for copper sent the price of that metal soaring, and it became worthwhile to reopen the Big Hole even though the only remaining ore was low grade. But the mining phase of Jerome's history ended, seemingly for good, in May of 1953, when Phelps Dodge once again discontinued operations there.

Today Jerome hangs on, a mile-high city straggling along the thirty-degree slope of Mingus Mountain. Its population dropped to less than three hundred at the lowest point, but those who remained formed the Jerome Historical Society, dedicated to preserving the city as a scenic and historical attraction. Their efforts have generally been successful. Late in 1965 Jerome was formally named an Arizona State Historic Park. It has become a colony for retired people and for artists and writers, and its population grows slowly from year to year. Two mining museums display relics of the boom days when more than $800,000,000 in copper, gold, and silver was being taken from the mountain. The scars of the titanic mining operations have begun to heal, and shrubbery is growing again on the surrounding slopes. An old-time hotel welcomes guests, and Jerome is drawing many visitors who are traveling to or from the Grand Canyon to the north.

Many of the old buildings are gone—destroyed by fire, like the Montana House that burned in 1915, or hurled to splinters by the landslides of later years. Most of those that remain stand empty, boarded up or hidden behind thick iron shutters. But in a nation that is coming increasingly to look toward its past, Jerome, along with Tombstone and other ghost towns of the old West, is working hard to provide a reasonable facsimile of life as it was lived in those nearly legendary days of long ago.

ELEVEN

The Last Ghost Towns

THE ERA of the boom-time mining camps of the old West was actually quite short. It began with the forty-niners and their California gold rush, continued through the next cycle of mine stampedes a decade later in Nevada and Colorado, and reached a climax in the 1860's when "instant towns" were mushrooming across thousands of square miles from the Dakotas to the Pacific and from the Canadian border to the Mexican. But by the 1880's an important change had come over the mining industry. Free-lance prospectors had ceased to make up the bulk of the seekers after buried treasure. Big companies, with their headquarters in San Francisco or New York, owned the mines and hired workmen at low wages to work them. The old free and easy spirit of the mining towns disappeared. In the past, it was every man for himself, and law and order were sometime things; now the mining company itself often owned the town and supplied armed guards to keep the hired hands—the miners—under control.

Something vital went out of the West when big business took over from strike-it-rich prospectors. The gaiety and liveliness and freedom from morality that had stamped the boom towns gave way to a somber struggle of employed against employer. Miners' unions were formed; there were strikes, petitions, widespread poverty, often warfare and sabotage. Once men had died in the mining towns because they dueled over women or cheated at cards or were careless and got scalped by Indian raiders. Now they died when company guards shot them for protesting the conditions in the mines. The old romantic era was over. The fun had ended, and profit was king.

But the West is a big place, and not all of it fell under the sway of giant corporations at once. There still was room for old-fashioned free enterprise that produced a few old-fashioned boom towns decades after the money lords had begun their reign. In these latter-day towns a man still could transform himself from a pauper into a millionaire overnight—and vice versa.

At the turn of this century the second Nevada mining boom produced a cluster of classic mining camps in the old style—virtually the last to go through the cycle of boom and bust to become ghost towns. The new rush began on May 19, 1900, when a prospector named Jim Butler found an outcropping of silver ore in a mountain-rimmed desert in western Nevada, about halfway between Reno and Las Vegas. Butler had gone prospecting with a partner, Bill Hall. They camped in the desert for the night, intending to get an early start in the morning. When dawn came Hall woke briskly and found Butler curled deep in his blankets. A couple of attempts to wake him failed, and the annoyed Hall finally loaded his gear aboard his burros and set out into the desert without him.

Butler, who was sometimes known as "Lazy Jim," woke a few hours later, finding that Hall had gone and that his own burros had strayed. A brisk wind was blowing, tossing the desert sand about and making things unpleasant. After a prolonged search Butler found that his animals had taken shelter from the flying sand behind a ledge on a rocky hillside. He sat down with them to wait for the wind to drop, and since he had nothing else to do he chipped a few rock samples from the ledge. Before long, the whole mining world knew that Jim Butler had found a rich silver mine.

Nevada's glittering Comstock Lode days had ended, and the state was badly in need of good news. Its annual gold and silver production had dropped from $47,000,000 in 1878 to less than $3,000,000 in 1899 During those years Nevada had lost a third of its entire population. But by the fall of 1900 the town of Tonopah was rising on the treeless, volcanic desert soil. Within a couple of years Tonopah had 20,000 people, and its mines were to produce some $300,000,000 of precious metals in the big years ahead. Though little mining is done there today, Tonopah is far from a ghost town. It has seen better days, perhaps, but it still shows plenty of life, and its growing popularity as a resort will keep it vigorous for years to come. To the south, though, are some former boom towns whose luck has not been so good.

During its early days Tonopah was not only a mining town but a center for prospectors hoping to bring in rich strikes in the surrounding countryside. For a while such strikes failed to materialize, although some crafty speculators in mining stocks managed to get wealthy on rumors. Many of these rumors concerned the area around Columbia Mountain, twenty-five miles south of Tonopah. A Shoshone Indian named Tom Fisherman had come upon a chunk of gold ore there in 1902. A couple of prospectors, Billy Marsh and Harry Stimler, found out about it and headed for the place. They located five claims in December and laid the foundations for a new mining camp. Since they were convinced that they were going to find the "granddaddy of all gold mines," they called their camp "Grandpa."

In the next few months nothing of interest turned up in Grandpa, and most of the early claims were abandoned. On May 24, 1903, Al Myers and R. C. Hart were working one of these abandoned claims when they hit pay dirt—Grandpa's first rich lode. They named their mine the Combination. About the same time a prospector named Charley Taylor arrived and visited with his friends Marsh and Stimler, who generously gave him a claim that they had already worked without results. Taylor struck gold and opened the Jumbo mine, after having failed to sell his claim for $150 to another newcomer. Over the next six years he netted $1,250,000 from the Jumbo.

Ten days after the discovery of Myers and Hart's Combination mine, the Tonopah *Miner* gave the news to the world with this headline:

SENSATIONAL STRIKE
IN GRANDPA DISTRICT

Every man not currently working a producing claim in Tonopah transferred himself immediately to Grandpa. Some staked claims of their own; others bought out the original prospectors. Among those who sold out were Marsh and Stimler, who let their claims go for $25,000. They thought they had done fairly well for themselves, but within thirty days those properties were worth more than a million. The stampede continued all summer, and by the fall eleven of the early arrivals were thinking about founding a town.

They put up $10 apiece and hired a surveyor to lay out sites. Instead of putting the town right on top of the mine district, they chose comparatively level land

between Columbia Mountain and Rabbit Springs. Here the town of Goldfield was born. The real estate promoters sold lots at $500 apiece at first; later on, land sold for ninety times that price. Those who could not afford to buy land became "lot jumpers" or squatters, seizing vacant areas and putting up shacks in a hurry. One miner, unable even to find a lot to jump, scrawled on the face of one of the town-site survey boards the message, "I lay claim from this point one thousand feet straight up in the air. Now beat that you damn land sharks."

Soon telephone and telegraph lines ran from Tonopah to Goldfield. As newspapers all over the West sang the praises of the new gold mines, a wild boom began. The Combination Mining Company shipped its first ore in December 1903, and a few months later the Jumbo,

Florence, and January mines made their initial shipments. Other producing mines followed. In the first six weeks of 1904 Goldfield's population grew from four hundred to one thousand, and that was just the beginning. The camp became a full-fledged town on April 29, 1904, when it acquired that necessity of any western metropolis, a newspaper. The Goldfield *News* went into operation that day, using a press and some old type that had been bought for $500. Its masthead declared that it would report "All that's new and true of the greatest Gold Camp ever known."

Goldfield produced so much gold in the summer of 1904 that a worried columnist for the *London Financial News* feared the possibility that gold would lose its value by becoming too common. He warned of a forthcoming "gold crisis" if Nevada continued to flood the world's banking system with such huge quantities of the yellow metal. In Goldfield, the real gold crisis was "high-grading"—or thievery. Miners hired at $3.50 a day were quietly picking up nuggets of gold worth hundreds of dollars, tucking them away in their overalls, and selling them. They scorned ore worth a dollar a pound or less as "company ore," and pocketed only the high-grade stuff. Some of the expert high-graders wore two shirts, sewed together around the bottom, into which they dropped attractive nuggets. Later they fashioned special canvas jackets equipped with pockets from shoulders to waist, and wore these under their shirts. Such jackets were known as "corset covers." Some miners stowed so much gold in their corset covers that they could barely walk as they went off shift. The foremen, of course, knew what was going on—but most of them were high-grading too. The mine operators did not dare to suppress the practice, because they were afraid of trouble with the miners; most of the operators simply leased their mines for a specific period of time from the mine owners, and if they got into a prolonged dispute with the high-graders that shut down their mines they would lose profits that could never be recovered.

There was plenty of gold for everybody, in any case. The Mohawk mine produced $5,000,000 in 106 days—not counting the take of the high-graders, some of whom were getting away with more than $2,000 a day. A single carload of ore from the Mohawk netted $574,958.39 for the company. A government report published in 1909 estimated that "over $2,000,000 was stolen from the Mohawk, Red Top, and Jumbo mines alone up to the later part of 1907," and that high-grading cost the Goldfield Consolidated Mines Company $1,000,000 in 1907 alone.

Nothing, not even high-grading, could check the liveliness of Goldfield. There was a momentary scare in the early months when a miner developed a high fever and a rash. Doc O'Toole, the deputy sheriff, thought the man was coming down with smallpox. Since Goldfield had no quarantine regulation, O'Toole invented one, and put the sick man under arrest on a charge of having smallpox. In the next few weeks he arrested one hundred and twenty-five men on the same charge, and then fell ill himself. In due time everyone recovered; it turned out that they had nothing more serious than chicken pox. The exception was O'Toole, who really had smallpox—but a mild case, and he recovered without complications.

The city flourished magnificently. The gold seemed inexhaustible, and each year thousands of new settlers arrived. High-grading miners spent extravagant sums for dinner at the Palm Grill Restaurant, which for elegance was said to rival the finest establishments of San Francisco, New York, or Paris. The corner of Crook and Main streets boasted four huge saloons and gambling halls, the Northern, the Palace, the Mohawk, and the Hermitage, which stayed open twenty-four hours a day. One old-time resident recalled, "When the leases were running good and the high-graders were stealing anywhere from twenty to two thousand a day each, and coming off shift every eight hours, you couldn't hardly notice the difference between three o'clock in the afternoon and three o'clock the next morning." In the Northern, where a dozen bartenders sold six barrels of whiskey a day, gambling ran into millions of dollars a year.

Goldfield had a more virtuous side, though. The

fourth issue of the Goldfield *News* announced on May 20, 1904, that "Next Monday the first public school in Goldfield will be opened, probably in the Miners' Union building on Main Street. Rev. F. H. Robinson has been engaged as teacher. The primary and grammar grades will be taught." An advertisement two weeks later told the miners, "Ice-cream and cake will be served at the Enterprise Lodging House from 2 to 9 P.M. next Sunday. 25¢ per plate."

Lawbreakers were brought before Judge E. R. Collins, who ran his court sternly. Sometimes the judge had to send his best customers to jail, for he was also part owner of the big saloon next to the post office, but he never let business interfere with duty. In the summer of 1904 the *News* reported that

Al Cook, formerly of Arizona, was up before Judge Collins this P.M., on a charge of disturbing the peace, court being held at Miners' Union Hall. M. M. Detch appeared as prosecuting attorney and E. Davidson defended. Both the defendant and his attorney were drunk, and the former becoming abusive, Judge Collins ordered court adjourned and the defendant remanded to jail. Cook took exception to this and threw a lamp at the judge's head, which barely missed him. The prisoner was at once hustled to jail and put in the iron cage.

The railroad line between Tonopah and Goldfield was completed in September 1905. Goldfield's population was then about 8,000. A dozen Goldfield mines produced nearly $7,000,000 in 1905, with the Florence leading the list at $1,848,000. The Mohawk soon surpassed it; some of its ore yielded better than $12,000 to the ton, a fantastic figure. Shares in these mines were briskly traded, and on October 1, 1905, Goldfield's stock exchange officially opened for business. Brokerage offices were found everywhere. One of them, the L. M. Sullivan Trust Company, was run by ex-convicts; it dealt almost exclusively in worthless securities, boasted that it employed clerks and stenographers to handle its business, and went bankrupt within two years, causing a loss of millions of dollars to gullible speculators around the country. More reputable was the firm of Patrick, Elliot, and Camp, headed by L. L. Patrick, one of the early investors in Goldfield's mines. Patrick said many years later:

> Business was so good that the first manager we hired stole ten thousand dollars in the first month without our even suspecting it. After that, it got better. All we had to do was get hold of a good property, organize a company to promote and develop it, have certificates printed for promotion stock, and advertise the stock in coast and eastern cities. It was snapped up. Frequently the whole issue would be sold out within a few days. Being a legitimate firm, with our own money invested in Goldfield, we picked out the best ground possible for our promotions and developed it with the promotion money. The investors who dealt with us got something for their money.

The L. M. Sullivan firm, by contrast, used its promotion funds to advertise the stock and never bothered to develop any mines. The stock kept going up as long as the advertising campaign lasted, which made everybody happy except the last ones to purchase the shares before someone noticed that the mine was worthless.

Goldfield's appetite for publicity was immense. Not content with promoting its fabulous gold mines, the town sought attention in 1906 by staging a prizefight billed as "The Battle of the Century" for the lightweight championship of the world. Tex Rickard, who owned the Northern Saloon and later became a famous boxing-match publicist, organized the Goldfield Athletic Club in the summer of 1906 to sponsor a championship fight between Joe Gans and Battling Nelson. Nelson insisted on $20,000 to risk his title, and Gans wanted $10,000 as the challenger. Rickard put up $10,000 himself and raised the rest of the purse from seven Goldfield business-men within a few minutes. All during the month of August the prizefight monopolized the front pages of Goldfield's newspapers, although a new strike of high-grade ore in the Mohawk mine got two columns on August 20.

The fight was scheduled for September 3, 1906. Thousands of visitors deluged Goldfield on the days just prior to the contest. The Goldfield *Sun* declared on the eve of the fight, "The streets of Goldfield were literally jammed last night with a holiday crowd of persons from all parts of the country and all walks of life. Trains rolled in at intervals all night, the last arriving at five o'clock this morning. . . . few of the excursionists went to bed . . . . Drilling contests preceded the battle. Waters and Hill of Tonopah drilled thirty-seven inches in fifteen minutes. That was followed by burro-races, foot-races, etc."

In those days prizefights continued until one man was defeated. So Gans and Nelson struggled for forty-two rounds under the desert sun until the contest was decided. Nelson struck a foul blow and Gans was declared the winner. Afterward, a carnival atmosphere prevailed in Goldfield as the hordes of out-of-town newspapermen, boxing men, and sightseers wandered from saloon to saloon.

The jubilee went on all through 1907. Nevada's gold production that year, $20,000,000, was exactly ten times as great as that of 1900. Goldfield, three years old, was producing $130,000 every twenty-four hours. The town's population was up to fifteen thousand and there was not a vacant store, office, house, or room to be had. Housing for ten thousand more people was under construction. Theaters, hotels, and restaurants offered luxurious fare. The situation was almost too good for belief.

Trouble developed late in 1907 when most of Goldfield's mines came under one ownership. The Goldfield Consolidated Mines Company, incorporated in November 1906, had taken control of the Mohawk, January,

Jumbo, and Red Top mines, and then the big Combination, so that it had a stranglehold on the entire district. The new company served notice that it would tolerate none of the high-grading and other cheerfully slapdash customs of the early era. Waste and extravagance were forbidden; Goldfield Consolidated was in business for profit, and let its miners know it. As working conditions toughened, the miners formed unions and threatened violence. There was talk of dynamiting the mine and shooting the mine owners—even of blowing up the whole town. A strike broke out in November 1907, and the mine owners convinced Nevada's governor that scores of lives and millions of dollars' worth of property were endangered. The governor asked President Theodore Roosevelt for help, and on December 6 the President ordered federal troops to occupy Goldfield.

When the troops arrived, though, they found everything quiet. The Goldfield *Review* commented,

> There is no truth in the stories of violence. About the only depredations thus far committed have been the pulling of the pumps at two or three mines. . . . Ever since the miners went out there have been rumors that buildings would be blown up. It was to prevent such trouble that the soldiers were called in. From some quarters there has been bitter denunciation of Governor Sparks, but . . . he has averted what might have been disastrous and tragic results.

A government commission heard the miners' grievances, but nothing was done to eradicate them. Most of the country was then in a financial depression, and jobs were scarce; the mine owners simply threatened to replace the striking miners with strikebreakers from other sections. The strike was crushed. The federal troops were removed, and by the spring of 1908 Goldfield's mines were yielding their customary bounty. The giddy anything-goes spirit of the town, though, never recovered from the harsh months of the strike. Now Goldfield's mines were run strictly according to business rules—and the fun was over.

Still the town grew. The population reached twenty thousand in 1910, and the mines, running in three shifts a day, produced a record total of $11,214,278. In that year the opulent Goldfield Hotel, built at a cost of $500,000, was opened. This substantial four-story brick building, on Columbia Avenue a block up the slope from Main Street, reflected the magnificence of the boom town. Its lobby, with mahogany woodwork and overstuffed leather chairs, was the last word in comfort. Half the rooms had private baths; the drapery was of velvet, the linens were of the finest quality, and thick red carpets covered the floors. At a three-day party to celebrate its opening, champagne flowed through the lobby and down the steps to the street.

But the splendor of the Goldfield Hotel was an omen; the town had reached its crest, and everything was downhill thereafter. The golden yield of the mines began to dwindle. One by one they tapered off—the Mohawk, which had produced $23,869,000 by the end of 1914; the Combination, with $13,175,000 to its credit; and all the others. Goldfield Consolidated closed the last of its mills on January 31, 1919, and moved the machinery to its mines in other regions.

The velvet draperies began to fade in the great hotel. The red carpets became threadbare. A sudden cloud-burst sent a flash flood rushing through the town, ripping away hundreds of houses. In 1923, when the population had dropped to half its number of a few years before, fire swept fifty-three blocks of the business district. Main Street was leveled from end to end. Every window in the Goldfield Hotel was broken when a building across the street in which dynamite was stored blew up; but the hotel itself was spared. The remaining inhabitants did not bother to rebuild; only a skeleton population still stayed, huddling together in the part of town that had not been reduced to rubble. Two more floods in 1931 brought more destruction, and in 1943 a second fire devoured all but the stone buildings.

Yet Goldfield struggled on. Its mines were reopened from time to time; its population hit bottom at about three hundred and slowly began to climb; a few new motels and filling stations were built after the Second World War. Today a small but thriving town, very much alive, exists beside the ruins of the old Goldfield

—and memories of the brief, wild era of that gaudy town linger on.

Seventy miles south of Goldfield are a pair of even eerier ghosts dating from that same era—Bullfrog and Rhyolite. On August 9, 1904, a prospector named Shorty Harris came out of California's grim Death Valley and discovered gold just across the line in Nevada. Shorty had been prospecting since 1878 without ever hitting the big money. Here he found an outcropping of gold in a ledge of odd-looking rock whose mottled greenish appearance led him to name the district Bullfrog.

He showed his ore sample to Ernie Cross, a friend of his, and they agreed it was a rich strike. Together they went into Goldfield to file claims. While he was in town Shorty got drunk and sold his claim for $800, but Cross held on a while longer, selling out later in the year for $60,000. Most of the prospectors in the Goldfield district headed south as soon as they heard of the new strike. Those who could afford it traveled by stagecoach for $18 or by automobile for $25, but most simply went jouncing through the roadless desert aboard wagons. Tents blossomed in the middle of nowhere, and when some lumber was trucked in from Goldfield the first shacks were built. The town of Bullfrog was born.

It lasted only a short while. The ore around Bullfrog was rich, but early in 1905 an even richer mine was discovered a few miles to the south. Its ore assayed $500 to the ton at the surface, which was better than at some of the great Goldfield mines. A couple of real estate men laid out a town near the new mines in February 1905, naming it Rhyolite after the greenish volcanic rock characteristic of the district, and talked the inhabitants of Bullfrog into moving out of their tents and shacks. Very shortly Bullfrog was a ghost town after only a few months of life, and Rhyolite was booming.

Rhyolite's big advantage—aside from the gold at its doorstep—was its water supply. Though it was near the northern end of Death Valley, in some of the most rugged desert country in the United States, it was served by nearby springs rising from the Amargosa River, one of the world's longest underground rivers. A water company was formed to pipe water from the springs to Rhyolite. It offered hydrant service and sold water at twelve and a half cents per barrel. An ice company supplied ice at five cents a pound, so that Rhyolite could lure prospectors with the promise of chilled beer after a hard day in the mines.

The prospectors came, and so did the wealthy investors who bought up their claims. Railroad lines ran to Rhyolite before long. The Southern Hotel, two stories high, with a lobby and bathrooms, was one of the first landmarks. Some brick and concrete buildings replaced the wooden shacks. One novelty was the Bottle House, a building made of empty beer bottles laid like bricks and cemented with adobe mortar. There were plans for building an opera house. Gambling houses, dance halls, and saloons multiplied; by the end of 1906, when Rhyolite had sixteen thousand inhabitants, there were forty-five saloons in operation and more on the way. The city also had three daily newspapers and two churches, one Presbyterian, one Catholic.

The Montgomery-Shoshone mine, Rhyolite's biggest producer, was soon developed to a depth of three hundred feet. The Bullfrog *Miner* declared, "Crosscuts have been made in every direction from the main shaft . . . and God alone knows how much gold and silver it will yield. The ore runs fifty dollars to three hundred dollars per ton. A great mill and cyanide plant will be located at Beatty [a nearby camp] for treatment of the ore." As the population soared and the yield of the mines grew ever greater, handsome buildings came to line the streets of Rhyolite. The most imposing of all was the $90,000 John S. Cook Building, which housed the First National Bank. It stood three floors high and had a massive burglar-proof vault. Mansions went up in the residential section, known as Nob Hill. A social group, the Women's Rhyolite Society, planned dances and charity bazaars. A schoolhouse was built in 1906, and two hundred children were enrolled—but no one had thought of hiring a teacher. By the time one was brought in, the enrollment was up to four hundred and Rhyolite's citizens were raising funds to replace the small wooden schoolhouse with a big concrete building.

Sacks of gold bullion piled up faster than they could be shipped to San Francisco. The usual wild transactions sent the prices of Bullfrog District mining stocks sky-high. True, there were some rumors that the lodes were shallow ones and that the bonanza days soon would end, but no one paid attention to such pessimistic tales. On through 1907 and 1908 Rhyolite's frenzy continued, and the Rhyolite *Herald* remarked in March 1909 that

Mid-winter, 1909, four years after the Bullfrog excitement started, finds the district enjoying the greatest prosperity in its history from a standpoint of ore production and mine development. During the year 1908 the district marketed close to one million dollars' worth of gold-silver ores and bullions . . . . The outlook for . . . the year 1909 is flattering in the extreme, and it is believed by many that the year's production will not fall short of two million dollars and perhaps reach much higher.

But quite suddenly everything came to a halt in Rhyolite. In 1910 the Montgomery-Shoshone mine had to close when the ore gave out. The lesser mines quickly followed. In a single year the population fell from twelve thousand to seven hundred. People abandoned fully equipped offices and completely furnished houses. By the time the big schoolhouse was finished, only eighteen pupils occupied its echoing classrooms. The newspapers went out of business and the presses were taken away. The $130,000 railroad station saw its last train some time in 1912, and when World War I began the tracks were ripped up and sold to Russia as scrap metal. "Rhyolite today perhaps is the ghostliest of all ghost towns," wrote a visitor in 1932. "The permanency with which it builded is the permanency of a granite shaft above the grave of the honored dead. Its stone buildings still stand, fronting on streets overgrown with sagebrush. Roofs are gone, windows are gone, interior woodwork is gone, ruthlessly looted for firewood by wandering prospectors who still have hopes, but not for Rhyolite."

Two decades later only five or six buildings remained, among them the concrete skeleton of the two-story schoolhouse, and the roofless, floorless hull of the bank building. The Bottle House is still there, operated as a museum for tourists. The shell of the jail still stands, but the gaping cellars and shattered foundations of most of the buildings are being obliterated by cactus and greasewood and sagebrush. The streets themselves are hard to detect. Looking at the ruins, it is not easy to believe that for six dazzling years Rhyolite was one of Nevada's biggest towns. Yet at least its traces survive. Time has wiped its predecessor, Bullfrog, from the face of the desert, and only the few local settlers are able to identify the place where once it stood.

Rhyolite and Bullfrog, born and dying in this century, are among the youngest of the ghost towns of the West. Possibly the youngest of all is Tyrone, New Mexico, which was founded as late as 1915. The fate of Tyrone was ironic, for it was designed as an ideal mining town. The Phelps Dodge Corporation built it at a cost of $1,000,000, hiring one of the nation's outstanding architects to design it. The architect chose the Spanish mission style, and laid the town out around a central landscaped plaza. The handsome buildings were erected at great expense: a general store that looked like a modern department store, a train depot, a bank, a post office, and an office building for Phelps Dodge. Colorful tile made the buildings bright and gay. In the railroad station a marble drinking fountain had an elaborate chandelier. Near town was a hospital said to be the best equipped medical center between Kansas City and San Francisco, and in the hills overlooking the business district were comfortable homes for the miners, also in the Spanish mission style.

Tyrone was a copper town. Some thirty-five hundred people lived there during World War I, when military needs spurred the demand for copper. The ore at Tyrone was low grade, so that mining it would be unprofitable unless the copper could be sold above fifteen cents a pound. Tyrone did well at the wartime price of twenty-eight and a half cents a pound, but after the war the copper price fell sharply. Tyrone could not compete with such mining centers as Jerome, Arizona. The copper company closed the Tyrone mines in April 1921, but kept them pumped dry and ready for reopening for almost a decade in the hope that the market would recover.

The coming of the depression destroyed that hope. The mine entrances were sealed, the railroad tracks were torn up to avoid the payment of property taxes on them, and weeds grew in the town's plaza. An attempt to transform Tyrone into a dude ranch in the 1930's was a failure; finally Phelps Dodge began renting some of the pleasant houses on the hillside to artists and retired couples. Beautiful Tyrone, which had had only six years of active life, became a drowsy ghost town with a population of about one hundred.

But in October 1966, with copper once again in great demand, Phelps Dodge announced that it was going to reopen the Tyrone mines. It planned to spend $100,000,000 to rip open the tunnels and create an open-pit mine covering one square mile, yielding fifty-five thousand tons of copper a year and employing eleven hundred men. Modern technology could make Tyrone profitable once more. After forty-five years of silence and neglect, Tyrone would come back to life.

Other one-time ghost towns elsewhere have been showing signs of renewed vitality. In the fall of 1966 the McCulloch Oil Corporation of Los Angeles revealed that it has revived mining on Smuggler Mountain, Colorado, near Aspen. The original Smuggler mine, discovered in the 1880's, was purchased from a prospector for

$50 and a mule. In the next two decades it produced about half the $120,000,000 of silver taken from the area around Aspen. Aspen itself became "the richest five acres on earth," with an opera house, six newspapers, and the first electric streetcars west of Kansas City. But its boom was crippled by the sharp drop in the price of silver in 1893, and eventually the Smuggler mine was abandoned.

McCulloch Oil began its work there by processing a million tons of waste material cast aside by the old-time miners. It expected to recover silver and lead at a profit of about $2 a ton, and then to enter the old mine itself, where 200,000 tons of commercial-grade silver ore were said to remain.

The deserted town of Terlingua, Texas, also faced the possibility of rebirth in 1966. Terlingua had been an important producer of quicksilver, or mercury, from 1891 to 1947. Spanish explorers had visited the area in the seventeenth century, and according to a local legend, had called it *Tres Linguas*, "three languages," because it was inhabited by Apache, Comanche, and Shawnee Indians. The name was corrupted later into *Terlingua*. Some mining claims were staked in the 1860's, but not until the discovery of the mercury deposits did any full-scale work begin. A permanent settlement was established in 1897. One man, Howard E. Perry of Portland, Oregon, owned the whole town—the mines, the store, the school, the church, and the homes. From a white adobe mansion overlooking the town he watched the operations on his property. He permitted no visitors at the mines, and the gates were guarded.

Terlingua produced millions of dollars' worth of mercury, which was shipped out in the seventy-six-pound flasks that are the standard unit for this unusual liquid metal. But after World War II the price of mercury declined, and when it reached $135 a flask mining ceased to be profitable at Terlingua. About the same time the mines there were flooded by underground water, and Howard Perry died at the age of eighty-six. The population of Terlingua, which had been one thousand in the best years and three hundred fifty at the end, fell to a single family, which stayed on to run a tiny curio shop and serve as caretakers for the town. But in 1965 the price of mercury rose above $400 a flask, and two large corporations began exploring for new mines around Terlingua. Continued demand for mercury may bring this little town, seventeen miles from the Mexican border, back to life.

Most of the ghost towns, though, will never again know the excitement of a mining boom. They had their moment on the stage of events, and then that moment passed. Some keep alive the glamor of the bad old days through dedicated programs of restoration and reconstruction; others are nothing more than heaps of rubble far from the main roads. The story of the American mining frontier can be traced in the ghost towns—from the camps of California's forty-niners to the twentieth-century ruins in the Nevada desert. They mark an epoch of high adventure, of quick wealth and quicker poverty, of gambling and gun-slinging and hell-raising, which cannot return. We who have seen too many western movies and television plays sometimes tend to think that the legends of the Wild West were all invented by modern script-writers—but the ghost towns remain, and their battered ruins testify that all this did in fact happen, that the legends are true, that behind the tall tales lies reality.

Bibliography

Andrist, Ralph K., *The California Gold Rush*. New York: American Heritage Publishing Company, 1961.

Atherton, Lewis, "Fire on the Comstock." *The American West*, Winter, 1965.

Bancroft, H. H., *California Inter Pocula*. San Francisco: The History Company, 1888.

History of Arizona and New Mexico. Albuquerque: First published 1889. Reissued in 1962 by Horn & Wallace.

History of Utah. San Francisco: The History Company, 1890.

Billington, Ray Allen, *Westward Expansion*. New York: Macmillan, 1949.

The Westward Movement in the United States. Princeton: D. Van Nostrand, 1959.

Borthwick, J. D., *Three Years in California*. London: Blackwood, 1857.

BOTKIN, B. A., *A Treasury of Western Folklore*. New York: Crown, 1951.

BRIMMER, LENORA, "Boothill Graveyard." *Arizona Highways*, January, 1948.

BURGESS, OPIE RUNDLE, "Quong Kee, Pioneer of Tombstone." *Arizona Highways*, July, 1949.

CARR, HARRY, *The West is Still Wild*. Boston: Houghton Mifflin, 1932.

CASEY, ROBERT J., *The Black Hills*. Indianapolis: The Bobbs-Merrill Company, 1949.

DILLON, RICHARD H., "J. Ross Browne and the Corruptible West." *The American West*, Spring, 1965.

EMRICH, DUNCAN (editor), *Comstock Bonanza*. New York: Vanguard Press, 1950.

GLASSCOCK, C. B., *Gold In Them Hills*. Indianapolis: The Bobbs-Merrill Company, 1932.

HAWGOOD, JOHN A., *America's Western Frontier*. New York: Alfred A. Knopf, 1966.

HOWARD, ROBERT WEST, *This Is the West*. New York: Rand McNally, 1957.

KEYES, NELSON BEECHER, *The American Frontier*. New York: Hanover House, 1954.

LEWIS, OSCAR, *Sutter's Fort*. Englewood Cliffs: Prentice-Hall, 1965.

MORGAN, CHARLES M., "Jerome." *Arizona Highways*, May, 1949.

NADEAU, REMI, "Go It, Washoe!" *American Heritage*, April, 1959.

NEIDER, CHARLES (editor), *The Great West*. New York: Coward-McCann, 1958.

O'BRIEN, ROBERT, *California Called Them*. New York: McGraw-Hill, 1951.

QUIETT, GLENN CHESNEY, *They Built the West.* New York: Appleton-Century, 1934.

RIDGE, MARTIN, "Why They Went West." *The American West,* Summer, 1964.

SMALL, JOE AUSTELL (editor), *The Best of True West.* New York: Julian Messner, 1964.

TWAIN, MARK, *Roughing It.* Connecticut: American Publishing Company, 1871.

WOLLE, MURIEL SIBELL, *The Bonanza Trail: Ghost Towns and Mining Camps of the West.* Bloomington: Indiana University Press, 1958.

Index

Index